Children's Digital Picture Books

During the COVID-19 pandemic lockdowns, children's media use increased (Mesce et al. 2022), while a decrease in print-book reading was observed (Nolan et al. 2022). An increase in tablet use suggests that when children were reading, it was mostly online in the form of ePub3 PDF files for illustrated works and prescribed school texts, while smartphone use was linked to apps and games (Susilowati et al. 2021). For many years now, children's publishers have experimented with digital picture-book formats but have regarded the genre as not suitable for digitisation.

This book documents the findings of a one-year research project engaging the children's publishing sector for feedback on reading trends and digital publishing in picture-book genres. The research assesses the plight of picture books in the current climate and considers how picture-book publishers cater to diverse readerships and new reading platforms post-COVID-19 lockdowns and into the digital age.

Written by an academic and editor with over 15 years of industry experience, this book offers a nuanced response to children's picture-book publishing and reception for librarians, teachers, publishers and international scholars in the fields of publishing studies, library studies, early childhood studies, early education and childhood psychology.

Katherine Day is a Lecturer in Publishing Practice at the University of Melbourne. She has extensive experience in the industry, having worked first as an editor at Penguin and then as a freelance editor for some of Australia's most respected publishers. Her research interests include editorial practice and author–publisher negotiations. Her latest book, *Publishing Contracts and the Post Negotiation Space* (2023, Routledge), explores author contracts and power relations between authors and publishers.

Children's Digital Picture Books
Readers and Publishers

Katherine Day

LONDON AND NEW YORK

First published 2024
by Routledge
4 Park Square, Milton Park, Abingdon, Oxon OX14 4RN

and by Routledge
605 Third Avenue, New York, NY 10158

Routledge is an imprint of the Taylor & Francis Group, an informa business

© 2024 Katherine Day

The right of Katherine Day to be identified as authors of this work has been asserted in accordance with sections 77 and 78 of the Copyright, Designs and Patents Act 1988.

All rights reserved. No part of this book may be reprinted or reproduced or utilised in any form or by any electronic, mechanical, or other means, now known or hereafter invented, including photocopying and recording, or in any information storage or retrieval system, without permission in writing from the publishers.

Trademark notice: Product or corporate names may be trademarks or registered trademarks, and are used only for identification and explanation without intent to infringe.

British Library Cataloguing-in-Publication Data
A catalogue record for this book is available from the British Library

ISBN: 978-1-032-74076-8 (hbk)
ISBN: 978-1-032-74092-8 (pbk)
ISBN: 978-1-003-46758-8 (ebk)

DOI: 10.4324/9781003467588

Typeset in Times
by Apex CoVantage, LLC

Contents

Acknowledgements   *vi*

1   Introduction   1

2   How Children Read   8

3   Picture-Book Publishing in the Digital Era   19

4   Conclusion   44

Index   *48*

Acknowledgements

I acknowledge and pay my respects to the Traditional Owners of the unceded land on which this book was written and researched: the Wurundjeri Woi Wurrung and Bunurong peoples of the Kulin Nation, and to their Elders past and present.

I would like to thank the School of Culture and Communication at The University of Melbourne for the generous financial assistance for this project, Olivia Campbell for research assistance and my colleagues in the Children and Family Mediascape group at The University of Melbourne: Associate Professor Wonsun Shin, Dr Sybil Nolan, Dr Wilfred Wang and Dr Xin Pei. Many thanks also to Bonnie Reid and Rob Sheehan for their editing and referencing.

1 Introduction

A recent 2021 survey of over 513 Australian parents and caregivers of children between 7 and 13 years old (Nolan et al. 2022) concluded that during the COVID-19 pandemic, children's use of screens rose, particularly in locations where long lockdowns brought compulsory homeschooling, and restrictions on gatherings and travel. For children, the effect of these new arrangements included increased access to digital tablets for school. This resulted in decreased opportunities for physical play with school friends and other children in their neighbourhoods, and decreased interactions with members of their extended family networks.

Increased screen time during COVID lockdowns also affected children's traditional reading, book buying and library borrowing in consequential ways for publishing and literature (Nolan et al. 2022). In Victoria, Australia, traditional book borrowing from public libraries declined, while ebook lending increased (Public Libraries Victoria 2021/22). The survey also revealed that tablet use was prevalent; while books were the most owned reading devices, tablets were a close second:

> Before lockdowns younger children (aged 7–10, n=277) predictably read more picture books (63%) and illustrated chapter books (47%) while older children (aged 11–13, n=236) read chapter books with no illustrations (67%), and school texts (55%). During the lockdowns, however, the data revealed that the younger children actually read fewer picture books (down from 63% to 57%) and more chapter books (both illustrated and non-illustrated). Again, this could be partly linked to an increase in tablet use, which would be an area for further investigation.
>
> (Nolan et al. 2022)

Picture books are not regarded by the trade publishing industry as a genre suitable for ebook format; however, increased tablet use for reading prompted further investigation for two reasons: first, to assess whether publishers had adapted their lists to meet increased demand for digital content; second, to assess if digital picture-book formats are likely to continue post-COVID-19 lockdowns, despite speculation about this format.

The study documented in this book reveals the findings of research aimed to engage the children's publishing sector to obtain feedback on reading trends and digital publishing in picture-book genres. The research assesses publishers' perceptions of picture books in the current climate and how publishers can cater to diverse readerships and new reading platforms in the digital age. In doing so, the following questions are asked:

- What proportion of the Australian children's picture-book market is digital?
- In the last decade, what digital developments have there been in Australian children's picture-book publishing?
- How often do children engage with texts via digital devices?
- Where do children access digital texts?
- Has the Australian children's picture-book publishing sector embraced digital publishing? If not, why?

The findings reveal that digital picture-book publishing is facilitated for most books as a PDF produced simultaneously with the printed edition. However, the digital children's picture book is not prioritised and, for many titles, not produced at all. This is despite publishers' awareness of children's increased tablet use and digital engagement overall. This awareness extends to other entertainment streams such as games, television and apps, and to an identifiable need for reading platforms that can cater to the needs of a diverse range of early readers. There appeared to be three main reasons for prioritising the physical paper format:

- That physical picture books increase the incidence of parental mediation and, thus, the child's heightened engagement with the text.
- That anecdotal industry knowledge indicates that parents and caregivers see the physical picture book as an antidote to screen time.
- That the picture book is perceived as a type of 'art form' that is best delivered in a physical paper format.

The study makes two further observations that may influence the rejection of the picture book in a digital format. The first is that picture-book publishers are highly skilled, experienced and knowledgeable in their area of expertise of producing *physical* picture books. Therefore, they possess concrete reasons for continuing with the physical format. Second, a distinction emerged between books which focus on visual literacy and early literacy skills, and picture books which focus on story alone. This suggests that early literacy books were more conducive to the digital format. For story-driven texts, the physical format was preserved. This is an important observation directly related to the increased use of iPads observed in the 2022 survey noted earlier. Preservation of the physical format also raises further questions about whether digital picture books are likely to become more popular as a result of lockdowns and the increase in homeschooling. Further questions arise about how the industry is adapting to this trend and/or if it will remain resistant to it and why.

A Historical Snapshot

The Australian children's picture-book sector has enjoyed a rich history since the earliest illustrated classics, such as May Gibbs' Gumnut Baby series, Norman Lindsay's *The Magic Pudding* (1918) and Dorothy Wall's Blinky Bill books. The formation of the Children's Book Council of Australia (CBCA) in 1945 began a culture of recognition and promotion of quality children's literature for early readers, and this culture was further enhanced in 2001 by the introduction of the 'Early Childhood' category (CBCA 2021) into the CBCA's annual awards. The CBCA was initially formed by two Americans from the US Information Library, Lena Rupert and Mary Townes Nyland, who were stationed in Australia. They believed the proliferation and popularity of children's picture books in Australia revealed that a celebration similar to that of the US Caldecott Medal would be possible and could elevate children's literature domestically.

The first CBCA award in 1946 honoured Leslie Rees for his picture book for older readers, *The Story of Karrawingi the Emu* (illustrated by Walter Cunningham). The award was conferred sporadically between 1946 and 1956. Afterwards, a specific early picture-book award was created and won by Peggy Barnard for *Wish and the Magic Nut* (illustrated by Sheila Hawkins). Since this time, the award has grown in significance along with the reputation of children's publishing more broadly. Subsequently, foundations and organisations that promote children's picture books have proliferated: the National Centre for Australian Children's Literature (NCACL) was established in 1974. The NCACL was first named the Lu Rees Archives, which was founded and championed by Lu Rees, Australian book seller, collector and children's literature advocate. The NCACL now contains over 52,000 books in its archives, and 546 research files of author manuscripts and illustrators' artworks. At around the same time, Joyce and Court Oldmeadow purchased Dromkeen Estate in the Macedon Ranges and had begun to collect and curate original artworks of children's picture-book illustrations, and manuscripts and other ephemera relating to children's picture-book publishing. In 2012, the collection was gifted to the State Library of Victoria. The annual Dromkeen Medal has been awarded since 1982 to Australia's most talented children's book creators whose works have made a significant contribution to the nation's appreciation and development of children's literature.

Dromkeen and NCACL collections display an appreciation of children's picture books and the complexity involved in picture-book creation from both creators' and publishers' perspectives. This creator–publisher relationship has produced memorable early-reading experiences and significant publishing lists in many of Australia's most respected publishing houses, such as Penguin Random House's (formerly Penguin Books) Puffin Australia list. Formed in 1981 by publisher Julie Watts OAM, the list included author/illustrators such as Graeme Base, Pamela Allen, Alison Lester and Gabrielle Wang, bestselling picture-book authors such as Mem Fox, and beloved illustrators Robert Ingpen (recipient of the Hans Christian Andersen Medal), Terry Denton and Craig Smith. The Allen & Unwin's children's list has celebrated the genre with titles by Leigh Hobbs, Margaret Wild and Ron Brooks. Both publishers have been recipients of the Dromkeen Medal for their exceptional contribution to children's picture-book publishing.

Describing the importance of these archives and the consistency of the awards in revealing the progression of the craft of picture-book publishing in all its complexity, Trish Milne and Belle Alderman have said: 'Here is the detailed story of the creators' journey, their relationships with illustrators and publishers, the progress from the first draft, and sometimes, the many iterations along the way' (Alderman and Milne 2016). This observation highlights the unique process of picture-book publishing as a highly collaborative activity. It requires specialised editorial skills to facilitate collaboration between all creators, and the skilful combination of illustrations and text. The specialist knowledge and artistry of children's picture books, however, have not always garnered the respect of literary critics.

Perceptions of Children's Picture-Book Publishing

While the snapshot above suggests a revered section of the industry that celebrates young readers, the CBCA still encounters criticism over its ability to competently judge the quality of children's literature; likewise, picture-book creators still struggle to assert the cultural value of the picture-book genre. This commentary is mostly based on two perceptions. The first is that the CBCA is comprised of professionals identified with 'primary school education and librarianship' (Macleod 2011). The second perception is embedded in the 'maternal paradigm' that historically frames picture-book creation as a female occupation undeserving of the same cultural respect as, and possessing less cultural capital than, adult literary works. As Garrison identified 'They could use their innate skills to make libraries more homelike, and were temperamentally better suited for painstaking jobs like cataloguing. Furthermore, librarianships emphasized feminine qualities of serving, self-sacrifice and high-mindedness' (Garrison 1973–73, 133). While this comment might seem shocking in the modern day, the perception of the librarian, in particular the school librarian, as a mothering type is a perception that still exists, steeped in the historical developments of early childhood literature in Australia, the UK and the US.

Elizabeth West describes the Brass Age of children's literature in the UK (the decades between 1930 and 1960) as being intensely active and pioneered by women whose primary goal was to produce for children 'good' books that were educational, entertaining and inspiring (West 2023, 3). While the concept of what constitutes a 'good' book is, West agrees, 'elusive and contested' (West 2023, 8), nevertheless these bookwomen employed specialist editorial skills from acquisitions to sales and marketing. They left a legacy by way of children's books being at least noticed at a time when publishing was dominated by a reverence for modernist adult literature (West 2023, 4). This is not to suggest the view that children's literature can only be middle-low brow has not persisted. Picture-book publishing as a predominantly female profession still attracts the pejorative and unwarranted connotations it did back at the beginning of the 20th century. This is despite the CBCA awards impacting the success of titles, and children's literature attracting a significant proportion of Australian book sales: in 2022, children's publishing enjoyed a 45.8% share of the Australian market with top titles such as the Bluey series (Books+Publishing 2023). Adult literary awards, by contrast, are judged by those who supposedly hold more esteem in literary circles (Macleod 2011).

The librarianship origins of the CBCA, and the sporadic conferral of the Picture Book of the Year, have no doubt created contestation if not confusion. Alongside the growth of in-house children's publishing departments (such as the aforementioned Puffin Australia list) and the general growth and respect bestowed upon children's picture books, a separation has emerged between picture books as entertainment narratives, and as narratives with educational value. The entertainment picture book, and the distinct celebration of illustrations via CBCA awards, has led to specialised picture-book production aims in which the art is given prominence. These aims include a clear emphasis on the visual appeal of picture books as opposed to older text-heavy award-winning titles such as Robert McCloskey's *Make Way for Ducklings* (1941), which won the Caldecott in 1942, and Annette Macarthur-Onslow's *UHU* (1969), which won the CBCA in 1970. Both these titles contain accomplished black-and-white or two-tone illustrations. The production values are sophisticated too. In their first editions, both were published as hardbacks with jackets. However, the focus on illustrative components and colour are secondary to the text. Shifts towards editing in which text and illustrations have a stronger relationship, and advances in printing and colour separation, have elevated the visual component in contemporary picture-book publishing. These developments have arguably contributed to the industry's perpetuation of the traditional format as superior; this has occurred despite digital developments in picture-book publishing which are mostly deemed a failure (Flood 2019) and reserved for educational titles, or produced as a PDF alongside the traditional format. The expertise that picture-book publishers and editors have fostered has been observed in digital developments, with the distinction between gaming and reading contributing to the insistence on the traditional picture-book format. In speaking about AI in books, with special features as opposed to PDFs for the sake of accessibility, Joel Naoum has said:

> I think the reason is that interactive storytelling already exists in the form of computer games. Publishers are good at telling narrative, and narrative has a beginning, a middle and an end. The bells and whistles don't really matter to readers, so I think ultimately the exciting and innovative part about digital publishing is about accessibility, the ease of distribution.
>
> (Naoum in Zwar 2016)

Delineating the digital experience quite cleanly as one that is not attached to narrative, prompts consideration of what digital texts are, and whether publishers adequately consider the relationship between digitality and story before conceiving of a digital text. For reasons of economy, efficiency or resistance, it would appear they do not. Before exploring how and why the industry continues to prefer the *traditional* format, it is necessary to understand the background relating to this preference. Chapter 2 considers distinctive differences between children's reception of digital reading and their reception of paper books. Scholarly research has revealed much about digital book preferences and physical book preferences, for both children and the adults engaged with children's reading. Chapter 2 also considers research findings which identify factors contributing to the perpetuation of preferences for the physical picture book.

References

Alderman, Belle, and Trish Milne. 2016. "The National Centre for Australian Children's Literature: A 'Unique and Significant Collection'." *Bookbird: A Journal of International Children's Literature* 54, no. 3 (Autumn): 55–60. https://doi.org/10.1353/bkb.2016.0088.

Barnard, Peggy. 1956. *Wish and the Magic Nut*. Sydney: John Sands Pty.

Books+Publishing. 2023. "Nielson: Australia Book Sales Up 7.2% in 2022." www.booksandpublishing.com.au/articles/2023/01/17/225222/nielsen-australian-book-sales-up-7-2-in-2022/.

The Children's Book Council of Australia. 2021. "CBCA Book of the Year Awards – 2021." Accessed August 28, 2023. https://cbca.org.au/winners-2021.

Flood, Alison. 2019. "'What's Taking so Long?': Children's Books Still Neglect BAME Readers, Finds Study." *The Guardian*, September 19. www.theguardian.com/books/2019/sep/19/whats-taking-so-long-childrens-books-still-neglect-bame-readers-finds-study.

Garrison, Dee. 1973. "The Tender Technicians: The Feminization of Public Librarianship 1876–1905." *Journal of Social History* 6: 131–159.

Lindsay, Norman. 1918. *The Magic Pudding*. Sydney: Angus and Robertson.

Lu Rees Archives, The National Centre for Australian Children's Literature Inc. 2023. "About NCACL." Accessed June 18, 2023. www.ncacl.org.au/homepage/about-ncacl/.

Macarthur-Onslow, Annette. 1969. *UHU*. Sydney: Ure Smith.

Macleod, Mark. 2011. "The Children's Book Council of Australia Book the Year and the Image Problem." *Access* 25, no. 1 (March): 27–34.

McCloskey, Robert. 1941. *Make Way for Ducklings*. New York: Viking Press.

Mesce, Martina, Alessandra Ragona, Silvia Cimino and Luca Cerniglia. 2022. "The Impact of media on Children During the Covid-19 Pandemic: A Narrative Review." 8(5): 3–28. https://doi.org/10.1016/j.heliyon.2022.e12489.

Nauom, Joel, in Jan. Zwar. 2016. "Disruption and Innovation in the Australian Book Industry: Case Studies of Trade and Education Publishers." Report. *Department of Economics, Macquarie University* (February): 1–314. https://doi.org/10.13140/RG.2.2.24585.03685.

Nelson, Bonnie R. 1980. "The Chimera of Professionalism." *Library Journal* 105 (October): 2029–33.

Nolan, Sybil, Katherine Day, Wonsun Shin, and Wilfred Wang. 2022. "Books Versus Screens: A Study of Australian Children's Media Use During the COVID Pandemic." *Publishing Research Quarterly* 38, no. 4 (December): 749–59. https://doi.org/10.1007/s12109-022-09899-w.

Public Libraries Victoria. n.d. "Public Libraries Victoria 2021/2022." Accessed June 18, 2023. www.plv.org.au/.

Rees, Leslie. 1958. *The Story of Karrawingi the Emu*. Sydney: John Sands Pty.

Susilowati, IH, Susiana Nugraha, Sudibyo Alimoeso, Bonado PH. 2021. "Screentime for Preschool Children: Learning from Home During the Covid-19 Pandemic." *Glob Pediatr Health* 8: 1–6. https://doi:10.1177/2333794X211017836.

West, Elizabeth. 2023. *The Women Who Invented Twentieth-Century Children's Literature: Only the Best*. New York: Routledge. https://doi.org/10.4324/9781003306870.

2 How Children Read

The value of reading picture books to children, and the preference for the paper version above the digital picture book, are well documented (Chen and Chen 2014; Stanica et al. 2019). Most notably, the observation of parental mediation as having a significant impact on children's processing and comprehension of texts has been emphasised and reiterated. Gillespie (2019) claims the benefits of reading to 0–8-year-olds include an increase in cognitive development and emergent literary skills. Wheeler and Hill (2021, 5) also claim that 'parents engage in a bonding experience that simultaneously influences language acquisition due to the natural discourse that occurs'. But what of reading on a digital device?

Since the Kindle, Sony E-reader and iPad were launched in Australia between 2009 and 2011, the publishing industry has predicted the demise of the physical paper book. While this has not transpired, there has indeed been some growth in the ebook market for genre fiction, adult non-fiction, and commercial and literary fiction. Children's picture books, however, persist in having the least successful transition to the digital format. There are many reasons for this, which stem from the ways children process texts (Pantaleo 2016; Sipe and Brightman 2009; Braid and Finch 2015; Bus, Nueman, and Roskos 2020).

Digital Picture-Book Reception and Early-Reading Experiences

Some literature about children's reception of digital texts is positive, such as Delneshin et al.'s study of reading comprehension between augmented reality (AR) and print storybooks. Findings from their study revealed that children reading augmented texts, with features such as 'touch', 'sound effects' and a 'storyteller' as an aural augmentation, scored higher in retelling the story and so had a better understanding of the story structure (Delneshin et al. 2020, 7) than children who had read only the print books. These findings are supported by other studies (Clark and Dünser 2012; Dünser and Hornecker 2007) which have suggested that AR in picture books encourages 'exploration of the story

How Children Read 9

contents' and that these features 'facilitated recall of the story, expand[ing] the ability to empathise and encourage active reading' (Delneshin et al. 2020, 7). The positive response to augmented picture books has also been observed by Furenes, Kucirkova, and Bus's (2021) review of 39 studies from 30 papers, which highlighted digital books outperforming physical books, particularly when enhancements were directly related to content (Furenes, Kucirkova, and Bus 2021, 502).

Parental mediation was also noted as a significant factor in children's understanding and reception of texts overall. While digital enhancements attracted children to the texts, the enhancements were also observed to be a distraction when children became fixated on the enhancement as a part of the device but at the expense of the story (Furenes, Kucirkova, and Bus 2021, 506–7). This distraction was also observed by Richter and Courage in their study of 79 preschoolers, which assessed their attention to the book (in both paper and digital formats), their attention towards the adult reader, off-task engagement and communication, and recall of story content (2017, 92). Supporting Furenes et al.'s study, they found the 'utterances that the most verbal children produced were primarily about the device and its operation during the e-book and mostly included labelling and comments about the story content during the paper book' (Richter and Courage 2017, 100). This observation was also noted by Lauricella, Barr, and Calvert (2014) and Krcmar and Cingel (2014) in their studies on the effects of hotspots versus no hotspots. Thus, parental mediation can assist children's reading comprehension when adult readers guide the child through the text to ensure they benefit from regular reading routines and the necessary scaffolding of narrative (Furenes, Kucirkova, and Bus 2021, 483). Given that digital texts with enhancements are offered to children because they are perceived as not having to be mediated, there is a risk of low comprehension in narrative-driven texts via the acts of pointing, clicking and swiping, which can affect meaning-making (Furenes, Kucirkova, and Bus 2021, 507). Delneshin et al.'s aforementioned study also conceded that while AR in picture books can reduce cognitive load via an active reading process that breaks up large amounts of text with multimedia content (Delneshin et al. 2020, 7), the enhancements need to be carefully considered within the story:

> Multimedia content which is only decorative and is not connected to the storyline, might play as seductive and irrelevant items that distract children from the story by increasing the cognitive load and interrupting information processing, so they may interfere with learning and do not add to the children's story comprehension.
>
> (Delneshin et al. 2020, 8)

The observation that physical picture books increase the incidence of parental mediation is true to the extent that it is more likely paper picture books will be read to children than digital texts. However, studies indicate that if the digital text is mediated and the storyline scaffolding guided by a parent or caregiver, the digital text could be comprehended more deeply by the child. This is especially true if the enhancements complement the storyline and narrative rather than the vocabulary (as would be the case for an embedded dictionary, for example) (Bus and Neuman 2009, 506).

Exploring Digital and Physical Paratexts in Early Literacy

It has been suggested that a nuanced approach to embedding AR in digital picture-book design has not been observed, and that 'due to the technical limitations and cost problems, the combination of AR technology and children's picture books is mostly tested in the market at present, and few products are well received' (Wang 2022, 13). In Australia, given the small market for digital picture books, sophisticated production is yet to be explored, and a lack of investment and attention to digital enhancements renders the format sub-par. Recommendations for better digital integration are therefore unlikely:

> When adding interface functions and visual elements, it should be fully considered whether these meet the standards of children users, eliminate irrelevant functions and elements, and reduce the thinking burden of children users. Adding complicated functions for the sake of visual effects will distract children's attention and affect user experience.
>
> (Wang 2022, 12)

Yokota and Teale (2014), for example, observed varying levels of digital picture-book technology: scanned printed picture books (a PDF), a visual or auditory design, digital features such as font setting, voice, music and hotspots, and interactive functions that gamify the text. The more complicated the design without consideration of the story, the more distracting the AR becomes, which can negatively impact learning (Takacs et al. 2015, 715). However, the importance of parental mediation again becomes apparent, and effective guidance can ensure children are not only engaged but immersed in the device at the digital features and narrative levels (Wang 2022, 12). Because children in pre-primary years cannot yet read, it is also important that they are guided through the experience of the picture book, and that parents scaffold the reading experience by explaining the various features as they are connected to the text. In other words, 'picture books are not for children to read but for children to listen' (Bai et al. 2022, 178).

In the case of the paper picture book, this also applies to the peritextual features that complement the book's narrative and design. The benefits of these features in children's picture books are also well documented (Pantaleo 2016; Sipe 2009; Martinez, Stier, and Falcon 2016; McNair 2021). In his seminal text on how paratexts declare to readers the style of a text, Gerard Genette wrote that the paratextual elements of a book – such as the author's name, the preface, illustrations, jacket, and front and end matter – 'surround [the text] and extend it, precisely in order to *present* it, in the usual sense of the verb but also in the strongest sense to *make present*, to ensure the text's presence in the world' (Genette 1997, 1). In the case of picture books, McNair claims that paratexts such as dust jackets and endpapers assist a child's aesthetic appreciation of a book as well as helping with comprehension because they also tell a story separate yet closely linked to the design (McNair 2021, 364). The illustrations in a picture book's endpapers, for example, might contain objects found in the book's text, which can be identified and discussed between child and reader. As Sipe describes:

> We should remove the dust jacket (if there is one) to see if perhaps the inside board cover is different from the dust jacket. . . . We should speculate (along with children) on why the illustrator, designer, or editor made these choices, communicating to children that every single detail of the book, and the placement of illustrations on the pages – is the result of somebody's calculated decision.
>
> (Sipe 2009, 15)

Pantaleo also argues that paratexts are designed specifically for engagement in this way: 'Conversations about peritextual features should be considered an integral part of the storybook read-aloud or literature discussions' (Pantaleo 2003, 74).

The intentional placement and production of these paratexts confirm the picture book as an art form that is potentially delivered best as a paper, physical format. Martinez et al. reiterate this view by claiming that 'in quality picture books a wealth of information related to the narrative can be found in the peritext – information readers can use to build a framework for stepping into story worlds' (Martinez, Stier, and Falcon 2016, 239). In the same way, the intentional placement of page breaks to add drama and build narrative provides a 'meta-fiction' (Jacobs and Bartow 2016, 359) that is a 'particularly interesting textual element . . . defined by absence; the picture book page break is a crucial part of the narrative' (Jacobs and Bartow 2016, 359). Unlike novels, in which page breaks occur as a matter of necessity, in picture books the page break is constructed and balanced with other sections of the book.

The page break and peritext of a picture book, however, are devices interpreted through guidance and use (Rumelhart and McClelland 1982), again emphasising the parent's or caregiver's involvement in the reading activity, which assists the child to understand 'how words, pictures, and physical aspects of the book are comprehended as a whole. Thus, while meaning-making is individual, it is also collaborative and guided' (Jacobs and Bartow 2016, 365). In doing so, the child can make 'linkages across the text, using the information from one page to make sense of another . . . refer[ing] to the image or words from previous pages using the clues to build an interpretation of the whole text as it [is] being read' (Braid and Finch 2015, 121). It is this attention to the design of the physical paper book to which publishers seem most attached, often elevating it above the perceived poorer-quality digital version.

Do Parents Prefer Paper?

Parents indicate that the experience of picture-book reading is a performance best delivered in a traditional paper format with expertly placed page turns and interesting paratextual features. For example, in a 2020 survey of 40 children and 48 parents, to assess sensory responses to picture-book design, Wei and Ma found that

> for both parents and children, the most attractive factor of conventional books is 'physical books' – indicating that individuals prefer this format because of the 'physical existence of a book', 'genuine sensation of turning pages', and 'sense of holding a book' (Wei and Ma 2020, 303) and that these physical features promote feelings of 'reality and ownership'.

Supporting this preference, a 2015 Australian Scholastic Kids and Family Reading report claimed that 72% of parents preferred print picture books for their children as opposed to digital books (Scholastic Kids and Family Reading Report 2015, 8), and that print was seen to be an antidote to screen time. The same Scholastic study conducted in the US found, for example, '81% of US parents of children aged 0–11 who had read both print and electronic books said print books were better for reading with children' (Common Sense Media 2013). The same Scholastic US study reported that despite '72% of US children 8 years and younger' having used a touchscreen device, the preference for reading, specifically, was for the physical paper format. This also applied to the UK, where in 2015 '75% of 3- and 4-year-olds had access to a tablet in their homes' (Ofcom, Children and parents report, 2015). However, digital-device use was reserved mostly for games and watching videos, and 'reading was the least common activity on multi-purpose digital devices' (Strouse and Ganea 2017, 8).

Strouse and Ganea sought to determine if the 'preference shown for print over electronic books was related to a general disengagement with electronic format books specifically or limited use of electronic media more generally'; they determined that due to the prevalence of engagement with electronic devices for activities such as watching videos, playing games and engaging with apps, 'children's lack of electronic book use did not appear to be based on an overall avoidance of digital media' (Strouse and Ganea 2017, 11). They noted that 'it is possible that caregivers and/or children believe that certain devices are "for certain activities"' (Strouse and Ganea 2017, 13). Their findings suggest that 'caregivers are not using the same adult-child interactions with electronic and print books' (Strouse and Ganea 2017, 14) and that 'parents do not welcome the shift from print to digital books and prefer to use print for children's learning, relaxation, entertainment, and parent-child bonding' (Strouse and Ganea 2017). These points confirm that parents appreciate print books as an antidote to screen time, which is reserved for 'screen' activities quite different from reading.

How the Pandemic Has Changed Early Reading: The Path Forward

Many of these studies, however, do not factor in unusual circumstances such as reading and parental mediation during the pandemic. The national survey cited in Chapter 1 revealed that the respondents' children spent more time on screens and that reading on a digital device was far more prevalent (Nolan et al. 2022). Similar studies worldwide have indicated screen time greatly increased during lockdowns when parents were forced to homeschool and work from home themselves, and children were unable to play with friends. A 2021 US study that explored whether parents were spending more quality time reading to their children showed a slight increase in the amount of time parents read to their children during lockdowns (Wheeler and Hill 2021). Likewise, another US summary of children's reading during the pandemic analysed the ways in which the COVID-19 pandemic opened new directions in reading beyond the 'for pleasure/for information' dichotomy. This summary revealed that because the pandemic kept most of the nation's children at home for a year or more, schools and libraries had to become highly creative in their programming and scheduling of activities. It also reported that reading activities of young people were ignited when adults in the family also displayed a love of reading (Smith 2021, 35).

With so many children pivoting towards screens, however, the question remains: which devices were most popular during lockdowns in the COVID-19 pandemic? Further interrogation reveals that children mostly used tablets for educational reading; however, for children's picture books, the shift towards audio was pronounced. Wei and Ma's 2020 study of the design attractiveness of children's picture-book formats emphasised audiobooks as being a 'particularly useful learning-aid for children with a low degree of literacy or learning disability' (Wei and Ma 2020, 304). They also found that audiobooks 'can be used for bedtime stories, especially when parents and children are unable to share this reading time together' (304). During lockdowns, audiobooks would no doubt have been advantageous to the parent. The question of whether the audiobook is perceived as being digital or 'other' is, however, still being discussed: within the industry, are audiobooks considered a 'digital' format? Did the shift towards audiobooks during lockdowns, via reading platforms such as Story Box Library (Story Box), change the perception of audio as a 'digital' platform?

The Emergence and Growth of Story Box

Although Story Box has been available since 2013, subscriptions greatly increased during lockdowns when it became difficult for families to access children's picture books from the school or local library, and authors started to record readings of their titles on YouTube and/or Instagram. The story recordings were produced with permission from publishers, who had relaxed the author contracts which normally do not permit unlicensed republication in any format. The practice became so popular and Story Box producers boosted their author engagement by paying creators and publishers a royalty fee for their contributions. At the beginning of the pandemic, Story Box recorded a year's worth of subscriptions in just one month (Alexis Carey 2020, news. com.au). It quickly saw an opportunity to also attract libraries to the business too. Story Box could be used for online events and programmes that would continue to engage library users during lockdowns, keeping the business connected both to local libraries and to their communities (storyboxlibrary.com. au, December 2020). Tracey Hawkins, Community Liaison Librarian from the State Library of Western Australia, claimed:

> Online engagement with Story Box Library (and in fact, across all of our online resources) increased significantly during the period when our doors, and those of many public libraries in Western Australia, were closed ... Statistics continue to show greater engagement than pre-COVID-19 times.
> (storyboxlibrary.com.au, November 2020)

Western Australia experienced several lockdowns that lasted only three or four days. This suggests other Australian jurisdictions that experienced long lockdowns, such as Victoria which experienced 262 lockdown days from March 2020 to October 2021, would be even more invested in online engagement with Story Box Library (Vally and Bennett 2021).

Story Box highlights on its website that removing obstacles to access to stories ensures children living in regional and remote areas of Australia and New Zealand, as well as children with disabilities, has been a beneficial and important outcome of the business. Additionally, audio delivery of a text can be an extremely effective substitute for parents or caregivers who have low levels of literacy, or who live in low socioeconomic households where purchasing expensive physical picture books is not possible. Accessing and experiencing audio picture books via libraries is a way for these families to offer their children all the benefits of reading outlined earlier.

Accessibility and Inclusion

Some countries are spearheading accessibility; for example, the European Accessibility Act comes into force by early 2024 in some European countries, making it mandatory to create a digital version of all text books (European Accessibility Act 2019). Other countries such as Australia lag in such concerted policymaking. In Europe, as a consequence of the new policy, converting trade picture books and illustrated books to digital formats will be helped by publishers considering accessibility through design from conception of the work. The traditional conversion process of simply recasting the physical book into an ePub3 PDF file can be improved if there is a strong design foundation for a better and more interactive experience for the reader from the outset, thinking of accessibility from the start and not as an afterthought. Given the boom in audiobook sales in Europe, editorial input into adaptations and various editions of the text while in production can help to facilitate different accessibility modes. The next step, then, is to explore what *is* happening in Australia regarding digital picture-book production, and what trends or emerging practices are in play to bring children's picture-book production into the digital realm. To ascertain the position of picture-book publishing with digitality in mind, I investigated the practices and perceptions of 12 publishers, editors and librarian/influencers. My aim was to establish an understanding of how those at the centre of the industry feel, what decisions they are making about what young Australian children are reading, and why they are making those decisions.

References

Bai, Jie, Hui Zhang, Qian Chen, Xiulan Cheng, and Yun Zhou. 2022. "Technical Supports and Emotional Design in Digital Picture Books for Children: A Review." *Procedia Computer Science* 201: 174–80. https://doi.org/10.1016/j.procs.2022.03.025.

Braid, Christine, and Brian Finch. 2015. "'Ah, I Know Why . . .': Children Developing Understandings Through Engaging with a Picture Book." *Literacy* 49, no. 3 (September): 115–22. https://doi.org/10.1111/lit.12057.

Bus, Adriana G., and Susan B. Neuman, eds. 2020. *Multimedia and Literacy Development: Improving Achievement for Young Learners*. New York: Routledge. https://doi.org/10.4324/9780203892152.

Carey, Alexis. 2020. "Coronavirus: Australian Businesses Booming Because of COVID-19." *News.com.au*, April 17. www.news.com.au/finance/business/retail/coronavirus-australian-businesses-booming-because-of-covid19/news-story/41e91a24c5f4b41c54fb97452b86a34e.

Chen, Chih-Ming, and Fang-Ya Chen. 2014. "Enhancing Digital Reading Performance with a Collaborative Reading Annotation System." *Computers & Education* 77 (August): 67–81. https://doi.org/10.1016/j.compedu.2014.04.010.

Clark, Adrian, and Andreas Dünser. 2012. "An Interactive Augmented Reality Coloring Book." Paper presented at 2012 IEEE Symposium on 3D User Interfaces (3DUI), Costa Mesa, CA, March 4–5, 7–10. https://doi.org/10.1109/3DUI.2012.6184168.

Common Sense Media. 2013. *Zero to Eight: Children's Media Use in America 2013*. Report. San Francisco: Common Sense Media. www.commonsensemedia.org/sites/default/files/research/zero-to-eight-2013.pdf.

Delneshin, Danaei, Hamid R. Jamali, Yazdan Mansourian, and Hassan Rastegarpour. 2020. "Comparing Reading Comprehension Between Children Reading Augmented Reality and Print Storybooks." *Computers & Education* 153 (August): 1–10. https://doi.org/10.1016/j.compedu.2020.103900.

Dünser, Andreas, and Eva Hornecker. 2007. "Lessons from an AR Book Study." Proceedings of the 1st International Conference on Tangible and Embedded Interaction, Baton Rouge, LA, February, 179–82. https://doi.org/10.1145/1226969.1227006.

The European Accessibility Act (EAA).

Furenes, May Irene, Natalia Kucirkova, and Adriana G. Bus. 2021. "A Comparison of Children's Reading on Paper Versus Screen: A Meta-Analysis." *Review of Educational Research* 91 (4): 483–517. https://doi.org/10.3102/003465432199807.

Genette, Gerard. 1997. *Paratexts: Thresholds of Interpretation*. Cambridge: Cambridge University Press.

Gillespie, Linda Groves. 2019. "Rocking and Rolling. Reading with Babies Matters!" *Young Children* 74, no. 3 (July). www.naeyc.org/resources/pubs/yc/jul2019/reading-with-babies-matters.

Jacobs, Katrina Emily Bartow. 2016. "The (Untold) Drama of the Turning Page: The Role of Page Breaks in Understanding Picture Books." *Children's Literature in Education: An International Quarterly* 47 (4): 357–73. https://doi.org/10.1007/s10583-016-9282-6.

Krcmar, Marina, and Drew P. Cingel. 2014. "Parent – Child Joint Reading in Traditional and Electronic Formats." *Media Psychology* 17, no. 3 (July–September): 262–81. https://doi.org/10.1080/15213269.2013.840243.

Lauricella, Alexis R., Rachel Barr, and Sandra L. Calvert. 2014. "Parent – Child Interactions During Traditional and Computer Storybook Reading for Children's Comprehension: Implications for Electronic Storybook Design." *International Journal of Child-Computer Interaction* 2, no. 1 (January): 17–25. https://doi.org/10.1016/j.ijcci.2014.07.001.

Martinez, Miriam, Catherine Stier, and Lori Falcon. 2016. "Judging a Book by Its Cover: An Investigation of Peritextual Features in Caldecott Award Books." *Children's Literature in Education* 47: 225–41. https://doi.org/10.1007/s10583-016-9272-8.

McNair, Jonda C. 2021. "Surprise, Surprise! Exploring Dust Jackets, Case Covers, and Endpapers in Picture Books to Support Comprehension." *The Reading Teacher* 74 (4): 363–73. https://doi.org/10.1002/trtr.1985.

Nolan, Sybil, Katherine Day, Wonsun Shin, and Wilfred Wang. 2022. "Books Versus Screens: A Study of Australian Children's Media Use During the COVID Pandemic." *Publishing Research Quarterly* 38, no. 4 (December): 749–59. https://doi.org/10.1007/s12109-022-09899-w.

OfCom. 2015. *Children and Parents: Media Use and Attitudes Report*. Report, November 20. www.ofcom.org.uk/research-and-data/media-literacy-research/childrens/children-parents-nov-15.

Pantaleo, Sylvia. 2003. "Godzilla lives in New York: Grade 1 students and the peritextual features of picture books." *Journal of Children's Literature* 29(2): 66–76.

Pantaleo, Sylvia. 2016. "Primary Students' Understanding and Appreciation of the Artwork in Picturebooks." *Journal of Early Childhood Literacy* 16 (2): 228–55. https://doi.org/10.1177/1468798415569816.

Richter, Anna, and Mary L. Courage. 2017. "Comparing Electronic and Paper Storybooks for Preschoolers: Attention, Engagement, and Recall." *Journal of Applied Developmental Psychology* 48 (January): 92–102. https://doi.org/10.1016/j.appdev.2017.01.002.

Rumelhart, David E., and James L. McClelland. 1982. "An Interactive Activation Model of Context Effects in Letter Perception: Part 2. The Contextual Enhancement Effect and Some Tests and Extensions of the Model." *Psychological Review* 89: 60–94.

Scholastic Inc. 2015. *Kids and Family Reading Report™*, 5th ed., 1–106. Report. Scholastic Inc., YouGov. www.scholastic.com/content/dam/KFRR/PastReports/KFRR2015_5th.pdf.

Sipe, Lawrence R., and Anne E. Brightman. 2009. "Young Children's Interpretations of Page Breaks in Contemporary Picture Storybooks." *Journal of Literacy Research* 41 (1): 68–103. https://doi.org/10.1080/10862960802695214.

Smith, Claire. 2021. "Reading in the Time of the Pandemic." *DKG Bulletin: Collegial Exchange* 88 (2): 35–37. https://research.ebsco.com/c/xppotz/viewer/pdf/w42asonunn.

Stanica, I. C., A. Moldoveanu, M. I. Dascalu, F. Moldoveanu, M. Radoi, and I. V. Nemoianu. 2019. "Emergent Technologies to Enrich Reading Outcomes Through Augmented Reality." *Revue Roumaine des Sciences Techniques Serie Electrotechnique et Energetique* 64 (1): 95–100.

Story Box Library. n.d. "Storybox Library." Accessed May 27, 2023. https://storyboxlibrary.com.au.

Strouse, Gabrielle A., and Patricia A. Ganea. 2017. "A Print Book Preference: Caregivers Report Higher Child Enjoyment and More Adult – Child Interactions When Reading Print Than Electronic Books." *International Journal of Child-Computer Interaction* 12 (April): 8–15. https://doi.org/10.1016/j.ijcci.2017.02.001.

Takacs, Zsofia K., Elise K. Stewart, and Ardriana G. Bus. 2015. "Benefits and Pitfalls of Multimedia and Interactive Features in Technology-Enhanced Storybooks: A Meta-Analysis." *Review of Educational Research* 85, no. 4 (December): 698–739. www.jstor.org/stable/24753027.

Vally, Hassan, and Catherine Bennett. 2021. "COVID in Victoria: 262 Days in Lockdown, 3 Stunning Successes and Four Affordable Failures." *The Conversation*. Accessed December 5, 2023. https://theconversation.com/covid-in-victoria-262-days-in-lockdown-3-stunning-successes-and-4-avoidable-failures-172408.

Wang, Rui. 2022. "Application of Augmented Reality Technology in Children's Picture Books Based on Educational Psychology." *Frontiers in Psychology* 13 (February): 1–14. https://doi.org/10.3389/fpsyg.2022.782958.

Wei, Chun-Chun, and Min-Yuan Ma. 2020. "Designing Attractive Children's Picture Books: Evaluating the Attractiveness Factors of Various Picture Book Formats." *Design Journal* 23 (2): 287–308. https://doi.org/10.1080/14606925.2020.1718277.

Wheeler, Deborah L., and Jennifer C. Hill. 2021. "The Impact of Covid-19 on Early Childhood Reading Practices." *Journal of Early Childhood Literacy* 1–20. https://doi.org/10.1177/1468798421104418.

Yokota, Junko, and Wiliam H. Teale. 2014. "Picture Books and the Digital World: Educators Making Informed Choices." *The Reading Teacher* 67 (8): 577–85. https://doi.org/10.1002/trtr.1262.

3 Picture-Book Publishing in the Digital Era

The interviews for this study were conducted from January to April 2023. Ethics approval was granted by the University of Melbourne for 15 semi-structured, de-identified interviews. The final interview count was nine interviewees (n=9) from a selection of independent and commercial publishing houses, and three reviewers/social media influencers (n=3) in the children's picture-book sphere. The interview participants were gathered from the corresponding author's own professional contacts from Australian publishers with a reputation for producing quality children's picture books. The social media influencers were drawn from the Victorian State Library's recommended children's book reviewers and an Instagram search of children's picture-book reviewers. The interview design aimed to analyse differences between the two interview groups; however, it must be noted that due to the small influencers group, this differentiation could not be reliably deduced to apply to influencers more generally. Consequently, the sample was treated as a whole group.

Interviewees were emailed to initially gauge their interest and then sent details of the study as a Plain Language Statement and Consent Form prior to arranging a date and time for the interview. Ten interviews were recorded online via Zoom, and two interviews were conducted by phone and recorded. Each interview was from 20 to 30 minutes in duration. The interview questions were grouped in the following areas of investigation: children's picture-book production, the response to digital picture books and their success in the market, what participants have observed about children's engagement with digital picture books versus paper picture books, library borrowing (digital and paper), and the future of digital publishing in the picture-book sector.

Picture-book publishing follows very similar production processes and editorial workflow across publishing houses; therefore, similarities between the interviewees' responses were expected and helped with de-identification. Additionally, the interview questions did not hone in on specifics of projects; rather, the questions were drafted with a view to identifying perceptions and market engagement with texts. The de-identified transcriptions were then analysed for key 'themes' relating to the areas of investigation

(Pace 2012) as 'a method for identifying, analyzing, organizing, describing, and reporting themes found within a data set' (Braun and Clarke 2006). For example, words and phrases from the transcriptions were categorised as being related to either 'text' and 'text development' or 'visual' and 'visual development'. Other themes were 'creation and production', 'parents and children engagement', 'children's reception', 'digital' and 'other' (which encompassed descriptions outside the initial identified themes). Within these themes, the words and phrases were grouped into 'positive' and 'negative' subset variables. For example, in 'digital', words such as 'accessibility' and 'interactivity' were coded as 'positive' and words such as 'non-viable' and 'gamification' were coded as negative. When necessary, and in order to provide a true rendering of the interviewees' intentions, the words and phrases were assessed in context with surrounding transcribed text to ensure accurate data labelling. Repetition of words and phrases was also noted (Ellis and Bochner 2006, 116).

Thematically coding the interview transcripts using the above method also allowed for the words and phrases to be condensed into 12 word-clouds (one for each interview) (DePaolo and Wilkinson 2014, 38). The word-clouds revealed commonly used words that could be compared across interviews and contextualised within the corresponding author's knowledge of the interviewees' individual publishing skill set; for example, an independent publisher versus a commercial multinational, or a publisher versus an editor. The findings are discussed in the following section.

Analysis

All interviewees were female. A recent survey from The University of Melbourne and the Australian Publishers Association, of 1,000 publishing professionals, showed that the industry is predominantly female (84%) (Driscoll and Bowen 2022). The high proportion of female publishing professionals would also appear to be reflected in picture-book publishing generally.

Overall, the response to picture-book publishing was positive: of all the coded words and phrases from the interview transcripts, 935 were categorised as positive compared with 376 negative words and phrases. The areas in which most positivity was expressed for picture-book creation, from acquisition to finished product, were connected to working with the text and visual elements of the picture-book genre, and the cherished collaboration between author, illustrator and publisher in this process. Many described the process as a 'marriage' and used words such as 'magic', 'marvellous', 'rich' and 'delightful' to describe the text and images. Of the process, some responses were:

> It's almost like you have a double narrative, like if you have a separate illustrator and author, you have the author writing the story and you have

an illustrator interpreting their story in a different way as well, which I think is a really magic thing to watch. [Participant 1]

The story has to be both accessible and yet have enough layers to warrant continued reading and be also pleasant to read, to have a good rhythm in terms of the words, and of course the illustrations are absolutely vital. So this is a completely creative collaboration. One can't exist without the other, really. So you know, it's an extremely wonderful partnership with an illustrator. I just love it because when I'm working on a picture book text I have an atmosphere in mind . . . it's a very particular skill. [Participant 12]

I'm always looking for something that will tell us about our culture. But even with a story that will move your view in some way – and that all sounds terribly worthy and I don't think that anyone wants to go to bed with a moral lesson – but you know, it could be just a funny story or a sad story, but just something that will resonate and shift along our understanding of our own selves. [Participant 7]

I think a book that allows them to be immersed in the story and provides a text narrative as well as a visual narrative is important. For a preschooler, perhaps the visual narrative might complement the text a little bit more, might be a little bit more literal. But I think for a primary-school age reader, I think the joy comes in reading the words and being able to decipher the story in a different way, or in a new, layered way through the artwork. [Participant 8]

These responses linked to the category of creation and production, and all related to the traditional paper format of picture-book production. The traditional picture-book format was preferred by every respondent for a variety of reasons. Notably, the book as art form and tactile object, and the shared experience between parent and child when reading the book, were the two main points raised by respondents in reiterating this preference. This is supported by the literature, which suggests that the paratextual features of a picture-book text enhance the narrative and amplify opportunities to experience the text when presented via the adult reader.

The Picture Book as Art Form Best Read Aloud

Two defining points emerged from the interviews. First, there was the respondents' insistence on the picture book as an art form: double-page spreads of proportionately devised, full-colour illustrations with endpapers and other paratextual elements that denote a sense of experience that cannot be replicated with the digital format. Second, respondents stressed that these production qualities should be delivered in a way that the child can experience them fully; that is, with the assistance of an engaged adult, at least in the first reading but ultimately continuously as a child–adult activity. The assertion from all respondents around the physicality of the picture book was passionately conveyed:

> People like to look at and handle a picture book when they are going to buy it. They like the object of the picture book, the production values, the art, the whole show. [Participant 7]
>
> The touch of the paper . . . you know, the shine and the thickness . . . I'm particularly conscious of, you know, paper stock. [Participant 6]
>
> A picture book is a tactile object, it is not just a book. It is a moment to spend together, it is a read aloud, it is a performance, it is a timed performance with page turns and rhythm and rhyme and it's read over and over again. [Participant 1]
>
> I love the experience of sharing a physical picture book . . . even just on a developmental level, the fine motor skills it takes to manipulate it, and the ability to flick forward and back and point things out, and pull picture books off the shelf and select the one you want. Like the experience of a physical picture book as object to treasure. [Participant 3]
>
> Babies and very young infants . . . they're not connecting with the book because they love what it says, because they can't read it and they're probably not even really taking [in] illustrations. But they're treating the book as an object that they then have a connection to. And I think for slightly older children who are able to go to a bookshelf in their home or in the library and pick out a book, and to grow up in a home where they see books, I think is really important not just for having that connection but feeling a sense of possession, feeling a sense of curiosity. [Participant 8]

These responses are consistent with Martinez et al.'s description of the picture book as art form, and Bartow Jacobs' identification of picture books' 'meta narrative', including the page breaks and turns. When considering these features of picture books in relation to the differences between physical picture-book texts and digital versions, it is these two points that consecrate the physical object as superior, according to respondents:

> In picture books every page turn means something, and that it sort of punctuates the story and gives it momentum and things like that. And it's not quite the same when you're just tapping the screen to turn a page, I think. [Participant 10]
>
> I think the visual thing of the picture book is not reproduced well digitally because it's more than just a purely visual experience, it's also tactile . . . They tend to touch the book a lot, they want to touch it, they want to run their fingers over the particular detail. They want to do all these sort of things, so it's a very tactile experience . . . If they've got a beloved picture

book on their lap, and they turn the pages and they touch it, it has the 3D experience, which then conjures up the world in a way which is different. [Participant 12]

For me a hardcover book (a) lasts longer in a school context and in a home context with young readers; (b) I think it makes it more of a special item. I'm all about making picture books be something that we teach children to value and care for and look after. And I think that a hardcover picture book has that weight and that tactile nature to it, which you don't get with the softcover picture book, and they usually have end papers, which I'm a big fan of, which extend the text and the illustrations. [Participant 5]

Immersive reception of these paratexts and features as contributing to the narrative, however, are reliant on parental supervision, which Bartow Jacobs describes as the 'guided reading' experience, and which the interviewees validate. It is interesting to note that the interviewees see parents as 'guides' and also as readers themselves, in the sense that they are often requested to read the same texts again and again:

Parents have to read that book again and again and again, and you know the books that you love to read to your kids. [Participant 7]

A really good children's picture book is one I think that both adults and children can enjoy, because generally speaking they are read to children by adults. [Participant 12]

They're more often than not listening to a picture book rather than reading it themselves. There's so much nostalgia for the parent. And . . . a lot of history: you want to bring your child to the book shop, you want to be able to touch everything, you want to see what they're naturally drawn to, you want to have your beautifully curated shelf to tell everyone who comes and visits you, look at how literary my child is, look at my beautifully curated bookshelf. I think that those sorts of things are always going to be equally as important as the actual content, at least for the parents. [Participant 6]

The success of the guided reading is contingent on the parent's availability, and their willingness and/or ability to engage with the text with their child. Interviewees' responses mostly did not factor in the chasm between enthusiastic adult picture-book readers and reluctant picture-book readers, or acknowledge that the specialisation invested in picture-book production is not always registered by readers who are not actively cognisant of the 'parts' of the book – the paratextual elements Genette describes. Rather, there was a general assumption from publishers, editors and influencers that sharing the experience of the book was a norm perpetuated from their own experiences of picture books when they were children:

> They want that experience of having a book, a kid on their lap with a book to read, in that old-fashioned way that they had as children, that is nostalgic to them. [Participant 3]
>
> I think that makes sense that, you know, if you have an adult there talking about the images, talking about . . . the experience, and being together, that's a big part of the reading experience for a child. [Participant 9]

One respondent spoke about their insistence on teaching children the importance of understanding the parts of the books, as a component of the experience of the physical object:

> I always say, you know, what's this part, the front cover, the back cover, the blurb, the spine of the book. What does the spine do? It holds the pages in, and look: some fell out of that one. And . . . this is the title, and the title is usually in a bigger font, and then we have the author and the illustrator on the front cover, and the author's name is first and the illustrator's name is second. [Participant 5]

While the benefits of consciously receiving the intentional placement of peritextual features has been described in this chapter (Bai et al. 2022; McNair 2021; Wei and Ma 2020; Sipe 2009; Pantaleo 2003), there is little data on reluctant parent readers and their experience of picture-book texts. Though the absence of this data might be due to a lack of active participation in research, it is a gap that could offer some context for preferences for digital reading or unsustained interest in physical book reading. Although many of the publishers and editors interviewed talked about their acquisitions processes as catering to parents who read books again and again, their decision-making is skewed towards parents who can afford picture books, who read themselves and who appreciate the qualities of the paratextual elements that contribute to the picture book as an art form. Another question arises about whether parents in fact still read to their children at all. It would potentially mitigate any consideration for special and artistic paratextual features if parents are purchasing books for their children to read completely independently. A couple of interviewees also noted the prohibitive cost of picture books.

> I think that there is a particular part of the population that is probably more high income, better educated, more likely . . . to be readers themselves, and therefore more likely to be kind of cultivating libraries for their children. And maybe then more predisposed to kind of acquiring books for their children and paying those higher price points. But I think

a lot of people don't have big children's libraries at home because they are more expensive and so their collections are built up through gifting. [Participant 11]

The adults are the ones buying books, so you need to appeal to them on a different level. And also, if you're going to read, a picture book is often read many, many, many times so you need to have different layers to it. So if it does have this, you know, both in terms of illustrations and the text, if it appeals to both the adult and the child it's more likely to be read again and again. [Participant 9]

There's even some picture books that I know adults buy because they want them for themselves rather than for their kids. [Participant 10]

When prompted to consider the limitations of some families to access physical picture books, and whether they engaged with them to any lesser extent during COVID, many respondents acknowledged that not all families are looking for books they can enjoy together, and not all families take the time to enjoy the artistry of the book. Some families simply want value for their purchase, to keep their children entertained. This was particularly so during lockdowns and potentially beyond lockdowns.

When you look at the picture books and early books over the last week in the top 40, most had ASPs [Average Selling Price] under $15.99. For us, our top 15 had 11 ASPs of under $15.99. So to me that would signal that the majority of people are buying in Kmart, Big W. [Participant 8]

But . . . maybe I'm coming from a position of being, you know . . . someone who loves books and who loves to share them, and knows how to share them. So, you know, not everyone is like that I guess. [Participant 2]

The gap between the kids that might have access to books and someone to read to them, you know, that seems to me to . . . be getting a bit wider. [Participant 7]

I think you can kind of look at it idealistically and think, this is a lovely book for families to read at night. But I don't think we necessarily think that every book will be read by a grown up to a child . . . I don't think we go into it thinking this has to be a book that all families can enjoy together. And we certainly don't approach the language in a sense of, you know, if a five-year-old wants to pick it up and read it they should be able to. But I guess we also don't think about picture books in specific age brackets . . . most of our picture books are probably for the ages of three to seven, we would say, so they're quite broad. And so yes, of course three- and four-year-olds are being read to. But the seven-year-olds might read it themselves. [Participant 8]

On this point about reading independently, during lockdowns many parents consistently read to their child/children, but a proportion of parents did not – their reasons ranging from not having enough time to their children being old enough to read on their own (Nolan et al. 2022). Reading to children tends to stop once a child can read independently – a milestone often embraced by parents. Continued shared reading experiences, however, were still encouraged by the interview respondents who reiterated that children can miss out on important cues without parental guidance:

> I know kids sort of get that confidence and then they think . . . I can read this by myself. But I think what an adult can do with the way they articulate and read aloud is very different to what a child can do. And it allows them to pick up on new vocabulary. Still, by that age they still don't know how to read every single word, and it allows you to pause and discuss things and just gain so much more meaning from it . . . I just think they gain so much from hearing an adult do that, even as they get older. [Participant 10]

Only a few publishers recognised that some adults were not very good picture-book readers. Oral delivery of a text does not necessarily mean that the reading is enjoyable. For a parent with low literacy levels, or one who is uncommitted to the reading (such as a working parent short of time and energy, for example) or lacking in theatrical expression, the proposed benefits of guided reading are significantly mitigated.

> There's a lot of parents out there that don't know how to read a picture book. [Participant 5]
>
> Kids who have [absent] parents, or parents who have to work all the time and can't be there reading their bedtime story . . . If you're not a reader or you're not into books, and you're really like . . . a parent who is wanting your kids to be read to. And so you get the book, a lot of picture books . . . they're not easy for . . . like we've got a lot of really bad literacy problems like in older generations. [Participant 1]

Further research on the impacts of passive or rote reading versus engaged reading would offer more context to the current research regarding parental mediation. Overall, there is a consensus that the physical picture book has benefits that ensure it continues to be reproduced in traditional formats, which can be enhanced with features that add to the narrative and experience of it as a treasured object. From the interviewees' perspectives, this experience is only amplified when guided by an adult reader who is enthusiastic, who is aware of the paratextual enhancements and purpose of a picture book's specific meta narrative, as well as versed in the various ways the picture book's features can be shared with the child. There are realistic limitations to the 'idealistic' (as one respondent referred to it) view of picture-book reception. This is especially so when considering the assumptions of parents' and families' access to books, and their abilities and enthusiasm as readers. However, the interviewee's positive accounts of the reading experience are supported by research, and feed into the importance editors and publishers feel about the 'craft' of picture-book creation, and their subsequent connectedness to its processes and longevity as a practice and product.

The commercial market and 'digital' reproduction of existing texts were the areas in which most negativity was connected to the creation and production of picture books.

Commerciality and Digitisation

The responses and descriptors in the 'creation and production' category of the data tended to focus on the pressure of balancing creative vision with market demands. However, the proportion of responses was positive overall: there were 105 negative responses in this category, compared with 143 positive responses.

As mentioned, the history of picture-book acquisition and production has been conducted mostly by women whose passion for early childhood texts, and aims for child readers, have created a specialised and nuanced approach to trade books. A child-centric focus, while worthy in terms of narrative development and authenticity within the storylines and central characters, does not, however, result in a book that children might want or enjoy. What parents want in a text might not be what children want in a text, but it is parents who purchase the books. Satisfying the entertaining qualities of picture books with the educational, or more 'worthy', aspects of picture-book texts is a constant balance that makes it difficult to define what a 'good' picture book is. Elizabeth West notes this balance as having been an ongoing assessment for those founding editors and publishers in the period from the 1930s to the 1960s:

> Quality in terms of children's literature was – and is – a nebulous concept, and although the desire to provide worthy reading material for the younger generation was nothing new, arguably what set this generation of librarians, authors and publishers apart was their understanding that children made their own demands of their literature. If it was to endure, a book must be picked up and read, and reread, and passed on.
>
> (98)

West also draws upon Eileen Colwell's criticism of the Enid Blyton books when they were first released as being popular but also 'ephemeral, their characters are puppets and there is no depth or sense of reality' (West 2023, 99). For contemporary publishers and editors the struggle continues. What they consider to be a text worth publishing might be quite different from what sells. Additionally, books written by well-known authors create added pressure. To tap into market trends and maximise opportunities for sales, publishers also try a scattergun approach to publishing to see what will hit a nerve with readers, as two respondents claim:

> It's quite a challenging time for picture books because there is so many celebrity authors. There's a couple of longstanding authors who have had a very long career, and their books will automatically be bought. But then there's a lot more publishers now in Australia so there's a lot more people doing picture books, which means the market is very flooded... There's such commercial pressure on publishers, like more and more and more and ... like redundancy after redundancy, team[s] shrunk, lists comparatively didn't really shrink that much. Like the amount of work, the amount of books you're working on, didn't really shrink. They got rid of most of the editorial assistants so now someone has to do production and editorial in their administrative wage paid job. There's just a lot that is not working in the publishing industry, paper prices have gone up about 100%, shipping has as well, and ... it is a much tougher market. [Participant 1]

The pressure is exacerbated by demand from book buyers, whose preference is still to purchase online or from the discount department stores (DDS):

> Sales are really boosted by the DDS ... So we're looking at what books are selling well in the DDS, who's going to be buying them, and thinking about our books from that perspective as well. So that kind of comes into it from the moment we are thinking about acquiring to producing the book, and then designing the cover, pricing it, doing sales and marketing. [Participant 8]

The responses to discount trade sales are backed by Nielsen Book data, which showed an 8.3% increase in sales in the children's sector in 2022. This increase was driven by graphic novels and illustrated texts, such as the Bluey series and Dave Pilsener titles (Books+Publishing 2023), both of which generate most sales in the DDS. Stock in the DDS also tends to be heavily discounted – achievable via the stores' bulk consignments and generous discounts of up to 75%. The cheaper price points for books from the DDS are attractive to savvy consumers who are not actively supportive of independent bookstores or who struggle to pay the higher prices in bricks-and-mortar outlets. Nolan et al.'s 2022 study found that most parents purchased children's books online during the COVID-19 lockdowns rather than from bricks-and-mortar bookstores, and that most of these purchases were from the DDS: of the 386 respondents to the survey who had bought one or more books for their children, 59.3% had purchased those books from discount stores (Nolan et al. 2022).

All interviewed publishers and editors feel this pressure as an unwelcome imposition on their work in picture-book production. Their determination about what constitutes a 'good' picture book, versus a picture book that might be successful but without 'depth', is firm but challenged by market demand, distribution, globalisation, digitisation and access. These factors are seen as external to the work of the picture-book publisher and therefore a distraction. These two poles of picture-book publishing also perpetuate emphases on 'the literary, psychological and theoretical aspects of writing for children' (West 2023, 3), which ignore the complexities of picture-book publishing in a broader context (Lyon Clark 2003, 14). When the creative vision for picture books is overshadowed by commercial considerations, publishers and editors expressed resentment and/or resignation.

Because publishers view the physical picture book as superior – experienced as an artwork and a creation – it could be assumed that the digital picture book would be mostly rejected. When collating the interviewees' responses, this assumption did at first glance appear true; however, as the next section details, publishers' feelings about digital picture books were complex. The success of the format was based on whether they could do justice to the production qualities to the same degree as their expectations of the physical format. Publishers and editors were open to digitalisation providing it did not compromise their expectations of quality in other areas of picture-book production, such as narrative flow. Another concern, which seemed more difficult to navigate, was how digitalisation impacted the child–parent reading experience. All these points are discussed in the next section.

The Digital Realm Not a Difficult Bridge to Cross

A little over 50% of the 404 responses to digital picture books were supportive. The positive responses mostly related to accessibility – the ability for ebooks to reach readers in remote areas, to be used by children with a disability and for children who require translation. Educational features were also noted, as was portability. However, the most positive comments regarding digital picture-book production were about audiobooks, and Story Box in particular:

> I love Story Box Library and other paid subscription services like that. To me there is still the sense of the adult reading the book to the child in that situation . . . You are seeing the text and you are hearing the words, so it's not a flat ebook experience . . . Story Box Library to me has a more human element to it . . . guiding the child through the reading experience. [Participant 5]
>
> I love what Storybox are doing and it's great to see the books having a different lease on life that way. And it feels a bit more natural maybe to have a filmed story time rather than a like a pdf. [Participant 8]

Some of the interviewees, however, noted that one of the limitations to audiobook versions of the picture books is that they are not long enough, unless delivered as a subscription-based portal of collections like Story Box:

> They're just not very long. [Participant 9]
>
> It's difficult to create an audiobook for a picture book given they're so, so short. Generally you only get picture book audiobooks when you can bundle them. [Participant 11]

Some publishers acknowledged the benefits of digital reading and that they were perhaps wrong to be sceptical of it when considering families from all socioeconomic backgrounds, especially those whose access to books is minimal, or whose engagement with texts for children and themselves is lacking. A 2014 study of 10,000 Australian children and families found that children who are not read to regularly are disadvantaged and more likely to fall behind at school compared with children whose parents read to them regularly (Growing Up in Australia 2014). Children who are read to have a higher vocabulary and stronger comprehension skills before they begin school and in the first few years of learning (Mol and Bus 2011).

> If there was, you know, a portion of the population who says we don't have the means to or can't access physical picture books, but hey we really love looking at them on the iPad, it's just that no one produces them. Then that's obviously an untapped market and it's obviously, you know, maybe that does show that publishers aren't connecting with their customers as much as they could be. [Participant 8]
>
> So much of the feedback is things like we need something for train travel, or we need something for like international flying, we need something for long journeys like from rural NSW. Like all this feedback about reasons why ebooks are practical. Maybe it's changing and publishing doesn't realise. [Participant 6]

Many respondents acknowledged that digital books created different reading experiences that are more accessible, including accessible pricing. Also, during lockdowns, accessibility was limited, and so digital books meant kids could still gain access to any kind of reading:

> There are lots of kids who don't have, who can't have, access to physical picture books. They're harder for them to read, they're visually impaired, you know, they don't have a book shop within 200 kilometres of where they live. Like there are all of these reasons why actually we do need to make different kinds of stories available in different kinds of ways. So that

all of these kids . . . different kids in different situations, can access them and not have to use purely educational materials, almost as though they were created with that . . . purpose in mind. [Participant 11]

[During lockdowns] they didn't have access probably to other books, they couldn't go to stores, they couldn't go to libraries. So you know, all reading is good reading I guess. [Participant 10]

A big portion of our consumers or customers . . . are shopping at DDS, and they might not have the means to go to an independent book shop, and they might not also be the types to go to a library. Like it, yeah, this might be the only way that they get books. [Participant 8]

You can find books everywhere these days and I think that gives families a lot more access too. You know, people who probably wouldn't go into a book store but they'd go into Kmart and they see them, and yeah access them that way too. [Participant 10]

Kids who need to hear language a lot more, perhaps they're from non-English speaking backgrounds and they don't hear it enough, and that's always a benefit. I think it is engaging. Kids like using devices and doing that sort of thing, and you know, they can offer a range of books to some kids that they wouldn't ordinarily have, depending on what sort of things they're reading or what they're accessing. [Participant 10]

There are obvious benefits to producing quality digital books, including benefits for children living with a disability, for children whose parents or caregivers cannot afford books, for those who cannot access or are not inclined to visit a library, and for those at home who simply cannot access books at all. Despite those benefits, respondents felt there was a consensus that the optimum reception for picture books was physical paper books. Respondents also noted that this perception was supported by booksellers. This raised some concerns around whether the impact of bricks-and-mortar stores, and the reliance on the publishers' trade with the booksellers, unduly informed their preference. When challenged by this realisation, some publishers even began to question their insistence on the physical book as the superior format. This was expressed as a delineation of the story, the narrative, and the vessel, the book. It could be surmised, for example, that the story is more important than the format in which it is delivered. This would render the format, then, potentially irrelevant:

> I mean my whole business model is really centred around physical books and particularly the children's books because the, hmm, I'm trying to think of the best way to say this. Yeah I'm trying, I'm actually, you're making me kind of question why we are so, yeah. [Participant 11]
>
> The book as an object, you know. We get a bit carried away with that, how much we love books . . . but really books are stories for me. [Participant 7]

One interviewee, however, articulated very clearly the shortcomings of the digital format, while still offering a balanced overview of the benefits of digital books as part of an overall reading 'diet' that includes a variety of reading material that can allow children to access and absorb texts in numerous ways and for different reading occasions:

> I can see the benefit of both. I love digital books because I think they break down barriers to books for students with additional needs in particular, and . . . have definitely broken down barriers to reading and I love them in that regard. And I think they are something that should be added to the suite of the way we access books, in the same way that I'm a massive fan of audiobooks because I think there is two things: access to story is really, really important and digital books are often a great way to access story. They're also more cost effective. You can get them free usually through public libraries and often through schools . . . so the cost is often significantly lower, although then you have to take into account the fact that the child needs an electronic device. So I think there's huge benefits to digital books and they should be part of a reading diet. [Participant 5]

However, on the same topic, the interviewee stated that:

> It worries me greatly that digital picture books would take over the picture books sphere. I don't feel that they will, but it does worry me greatly. I don't think there's enough education for parents in particular, and probably teachers, around the education that still needs to go into reading a digital book . . . we assume that these kids are digital natives. I don't think we can assume that they know how to use a digital book and get as much out of it. [Participant 5]

This comment promotes again the parent as the mediator of the text and the likelihood that the parent will be more accustomed to the physical format (based on their own childhood reading experiences as well as the prevalence of physical picture books in the market). The likelihood of the digital format being navigated by the child user without parental mediation, perhaps due to features that offer some form of guided reading – bells to turn the page, audio elements such as pre-recorded voiceover, or other features that allow a child to flip, tap or zoom to different elements of the page layout, is indicated. As noted in the previous chapter, however, it is the presence of such elements that have the potential to also distract children from the narrative arc of the story (Furenes, Kucirkova, and Bus 2021, 506). These observations also play into publishers' fears that digitisation is changing the picture book in ways that aren't aligned with the original aims of picture books in terms of how publishers see them:

> It's gamification of reading. [Participant 5]
>
> A picture book isn't about add-ins. It's about what is in the book. And if you start doing add-in[s] it becomes an app, or becomes something else. It doesn't remain a picture book. [Participant 1]
>
> I don't 100% know, but my assumption is that digital children's picture books are often used in the same way that we might use YouTube. They're a babysitting device. [Participant 5]

And yet, a lack of interactive elements is also considered problematic, too. In some interviewees' opinions, the digital format should promote a reading experience vastly different from the physical book, and that if it does not, then what is the point:

> From my personal point of view I think a digital picture book should be more than just turning the pages on a PDF. And so then it comes down to, was that the movement that we saw in 2010–11 and the likes of *Nosy Crow*? Really putting a lot of effort into those kind of apps. And has that movement passed now? Yes, I think those kind of questions come up. But I just keep thinking about how small our team is, and how stretched for time we are already, and how that would fit in, and how we would sort of be able to justify to the higher-ups to produce something without very hard data. [Participant 8]

There was a strong sense that one of the reasons publishers and editors did not embrace the digital format was the lack of control with how the object is used. Picture-book creators, as noted, put a lot of planning and thought into the physical format, and how it is read and absorbed. The scale and placement of the illustrations and text, as well as the design of the end-papers, choice of stock and dimensions of the book, encourage readers to experience the text in a very directed way. While no publisher can be certain that the text will be read in the way they anticipate, the traditional format does present some hidden rules as to how it should be enjoyed simply via its front-to-back embodiment. This is not necessarily the case for a digital format when it can be manipulated in the ways mentioned earlier, as one respondent noted:

> I think, as an illustrated publisher, the user experiences are very important to us. We like to have a bit more control over it, about how the design looks, where people are seeing it, how the images look. And especially in

pre-production we do so many, so much colour proofing. And to feel like you lose that control right at the end has probably been why we've stayed away from, I guess, digital formats. [Participant 6]

I feel like if you're going to do it where you just do a pdf, you can't control what people are viewing it on. They're not going to have the same experience because if they're trying to read it on a little screen and it's a big double page spread. And I feel like with picture books it's all about the timing and the scale. [Participant 1]

It makes us feel like we're going to lose more control unless we can do it properly. So you know, something like the production assistant who at the moment digitises the books has no experience in it. So maybe that's a point, like if we had an in-house designer who could have a little bit more control over making sure that that fixed format is going to look good. [Participant 6]

These reactions only partly stem from publishers' lack of skills in digital picture-book production; their resistance cannot be solely attributed to their preferences for the physical format. With booksellers cornering a huge market for physical books, and with publishers relying on a B2B model, whereby booksellers are central to the sales success of titles, the extremely small numbers of digital sales do not afford publishers the luxury of experimentation:

Knowing how small we are as a team, knowing the kind of good relationships that we have with retailers, that we have sales team reps going out across the country, I don't know if digital would be something that we would explore. [Participant 8]

It's very tiny. I want to say like even less than 5%. I think in a good month leading up to Christmas, we were doing maybe 150 to 200 ebooks a month. [Participant 6]

The demand was not incredibly significant even during COVID. You know, as a percentage of book sales it was minuscule. [Participant 12]

The backend as well to produce them would be quite sophisticated. And whether or not we would have those kind of resources on top of the other considerations, yeah I just couldn't . . . see us doing it.

Nobody, but I mean nobody, buys them. I mean our sales numbers are very small . . . Two per cent of our books are purchased as ebooks. [Participant 11]

Since the introduction of ebooks to the Australian market, many have prophesied the demise of the physical book. Ebooks have not had the success that was expected, however. Print books are still the preferred format in

Australia, especially for books with illustrative content such as coffee-table books, cookbooks and children's picture books, but also even for mono books that are the most transferrable. Booksellers' investment in print books as consumer items sold through bricks-and-mortar stores is therefore only part of the problem. Certainly this business model contributes to readers' exposure to books as being predominantly print, but the unenthusiastic adoption of ebooks has consecrated publishers' feelings that some books are better in a physical format: for the way in which art and illustration can be presented and displayed; for the experience of engaging in the 'parts' of the book; and for the picture book as a vehicle for child–parent engagement. To further support this belief, a lack of skill in the technology and design of ebooks means that picture books are only ever released as a PDF of the original print copy. Many feel that this is vastly inferior and not worth the investment:

> We did do a trial recently with about three or four, illustrated books, which we don't know went as well. So with the illustrated books you can't have a free-flowing format. So we're doing a fixed format which is around $600, takes at least two hours, maybe two to three hours, for the production assistant to organise, and with that the user experience isn't as nice. So you know, you've got a page where there could be multiple images, also captions, and also text, and unfortunately you can't resize any of that. You can only zoom in onto the page, so the user sort of has to navigate their way around. The other problem is, in illustrated, everything is in colour and so often a lot of the older devices don't accommodate colour, so that is also another thing that's not a great experience. [Participant 6]
>
> Ebooks really do need careful curation and you know, monitoring of price points, and making good use of past promotions to kind of push them up the charts and get them to a point where they're taken notice of by book buyers who are sort of browsing. [Participant 11]
>
> I just I think we are a pretty small publisher and so the capacity to make them really high quality needs a different level of . . . I would probably have the expertise but just the workload of doing it all, and there might be quicker ways of doing it now. [Participant 1]

A lack of in-house resources is also part of the problem. Many publishers and editors feel their expertise of picture-book creation does not extend to creating digital reading experiences, which they perceive as a skill quite separate to the ways in which picture books have traditionally been produced. These print-production skills are not transferrable; or rather, the digital experience cannot be integrated into the traditional production of the print model. This is partly to do with an absence of knowledge, but also a sense of resistance to the digital format because of the cost. Many of the interviewees conveyed how their investment was minimal when considering and employing digital features into books, or conceiving of digital productions of picture books:

> Publishing people aren't good at making digital stuff in the way that digital people are. Like we do books well, and the digital stuff we made was clunky and not nearly as slick . . . So whether or not that changes when you have a whole generation of editors and publishers who are digital natives, and they've got really good ideas about using this space. But for the moment it seems pretty much like they're in different lanes and they're not going to converge any time soon . . . That's completely done by a completely different department. I don't know, I never even see them. The editor approves them, but they're sort of done very much in the background because the sales of them are so small that they're kind of considered something that's done off to the side . . . Why are we even trying? We are embarrassing ourselves, really. [Participant 3]

Publishers' reasons for not investing in digital appear just as much practical as ideological. Their concern about the picture-book-reading experience being compromised is justifiable considering the lack of investment – both monetary and in skills – to ensure digital picture books offer the expected level of excellence. It is difficult to gauge whether the publishers have made any concerted attempt to investigate this area of publishing. A lack of sales certainly contributes to the dilemma. Many publishers and parents also see picture books as an antidote to screen time, even if they feel that this belief is anecdotal only. This antidote to screen time is discussed in the following section.

If They Are Reading, Then They Are Not on Screens

As Strouse et al. discovered in their study mentioned in Chapter 2, children's lack of engagement with ebooks did not indicate a lack of interest in digital devices at all (2017, 11). Rather, children's digital engagement was reserved for activities most conducive to, and conceived in, a digital format, including gaming, watching television or for interactive learning via apps. The parents in Strouse et al.'s study preferred print books for their ability to extract children from devices and experience entertainment and relaxation in different ways. There was also an emphasis on child–parent/guardian engagement. Respondents said they did not engage with their children when they used digital devices; therefore, physical books were preferred because they facilitated interaction (14).

It should be noted that Strouse et al.'s study was performed before the pandemic, which has undoubtedly shifted people's perceptions of acceptable digital use. When everyone was forced into lockdown, working from home and communicating with friends, colleagues and family members meant we used digital devices more. The proportion of time spent on digital devices has increased since lockdowns, too, and it is also possible that reading has shifted alongside this trend. It is yet to be revealed whether children's sustained use of digital media will continue or go back to what it was pre-pandemic. Increased use is, perhaps, one reason for parents to insist on print picture books as an antidote to digital media. Therefore, it would appear unlikely that increased use of digital media would persuade publishers and parents/caregivers that children's picture books should be produced more frequently in a digital format. This was reflected in the interviewees' responses, particularly when regarding their own children's digital media use (if they had children). Respondents also reflected on how physical books are absorbed quite differently from digital texts and that the reception of the physical object should be preserved. Again, they offered this view as anecdotal rather than based on any evidence via research or statistics:

> I know again it's anecdotal evidence but I think this is kind of borne out with the limited research that we've done into this, it is that screen time is for TV. My kids are too young for computers. But when you're kind of balancing requests for TV and, you know, computer and using or borrowing your iPhone for a game or whatever. The idea of then taking reading time which is kind of sacrosanct and an opportunity for connection and with educational. It's really hard to feel like you want to turn that into screen time too. It's supposed to be its own special thing. [Participant 11]
>
> To them, the screen is either about school work or it's about social stuff, and so it's not something that they associate with pleasure. [Participant 12]
>
> I think having the child feel like reading . . . it happens not just on the screen, because they do so many things on the screen all the time, and reading can be different from that. [Participant 9]
>
> We're trying to get kids off screen, and particularly at night when most picture books are read, you don't want to have the iPad out. And you want to be transitioning away from screens. [Participant 6]
>
> Yeah, I think they read differently. I think they take in the information differently. And I think they spend so much time looking at a screen that it's just nice to get away from that. And I wonder whether the picture book, digital picture books, haven't really taken off because, you know, your gatekeepers like your librarians and your parents want to see kids reading physical books rather than books online. [Participant 2]
>
> Parents are worried about screen time for their kids. They don't want to introduce it if they don't have to. [Participant 3]
>
> Their [the parents'] preference is that their children are reading a physical book because they spend so much time on screens, and they spent so

much time on screens during lockdown that certainly they want them off screens now. [Participant 5]

For me the physical book is very much a reminder that this is my time to read. I'm setting aside this time to read. I'm going to be mindful about this and intentional about reading. Whereas it's very easy to flick in and out of digital books and, you know, the sustained attention just to me isn't there. [Participant 5]

This last comment relates back to the physical picture book's paratextual signifiers which direct readers through the reading experience. Distractions via illustrations or text form part of the discussion of a story rather than being oblique to the text, like a hotspot that might take the reader to an area of investigation outside the narrative. As one respondent quoted earlier said, 'It's gamification of reading'. Any significant shift to considerably produce digital picture books, therefore, is not likely to happen anytime soon. This is for reasons quite separate from publishers' insistence on physical picture books being superior alone; rather, it is the combination of years of traditional production knowledge and expertise, which publishers and editors are reluctant to depart from, the market framework being highly reliant on a bricks-and-mortar business model, and the perception that picture books are an antidote to digital interaction, which is still seen to be related to specific activities that do not include reading.

There is one area where a digital experience links well with reading, and that is in educational publishing. Educational publishing is Australia's largest book market, 'representing over 41% of books sold and generat[ing] approximately $62 million in revenue export annually' (IBIS World 2023). Competition in the educational market is robust and the sector has been the first to pivot towards digital delivery. This was first instigated via CD-ROM, but now includes apps, ebooks and other digital platforms for independent learning and classroom activities.

Picture-Book Publishing Is Different From Educational Publishing

As noted in Chapter 2, in-built features of a digital text have received mixed reception dependent on the extent of narrative in the text, and whether the narrative is to be read in a linear fashion or not. For texts that offer features that pull the reader away from a story, such as built-in dictionaries, sound effects and pop-ups, the danger is in the reader not navigating through the story in the way the author intended. In the worst-case scenario this means that the reader cannot comprehend the text and therefore misses out on important messages and experiences. However, if the additional digital features of a text supplement its resource-like premise, then these features can enhance the reading experience (Delneshin et al. 2020) both in texts that children read independently and in non-narrative-driven texts.

The creative children's picture book (i.e. one that relies more on story than education) has criteria that resist digital enhancement and promote linear reading and a shared reading experience (that between a child and their parent or a guardian). This is an important distinction to make because it underpins, from a book publisher's perspective, decisions around digital formats and how the text can be adapted to suit this delivery: that is, does the text provide a narrative that is amenable to an in-built dictionary? Will the narrative be too disrupted by augmentation that distracts the child reader from the narrative thread?

Published in 2010, Oliver Jeffers' *The Heart and the Bottle*, was one of the first Australian picture books to be produced as an app. The features included opening picture frames, falling snow and audio augmentation. While the features were expertly produced and the majority of reviews of the app favourable, there was criticism of the necessity to prompt the features and, in doing so, lose the thread of the linear story (Kirkus Reviews 2011). Educational publishing, by contrast, can be seen to embrace features in reading because they are primarily reference-focused. As one respondent in the interviews noted:

> I feel like this is where publishing and picture books verge away from each other. Like educational books absolutely, absolutely they should have digital picture books for education. [Participant 1]

Also, according to the interview respondents in this study, the physical children's picture book was considered an antidote to *anything* digital (whether that is a digital picture book, online game or free-to-air television). This is certainly a reason why both picture-book producers and parents resist digitalising books. It might be one of the only remaining forms of entertainment for children that is not digital. The educational book can be separated quite clearly from the aspirational, story-led picture book, which can sometimes offer more intangible qualities that can be absorbed by the readers as an appreciation of a unique work, in turn separating unique works from pedestrian types of writing, as Colwell describes:

> Style cannot be defined in the language of grammar and syntax. It is concerned with the choice of words and the way in which they are used. It can be heard by the ear and appreciated by the intellect. It stamps a book as the work of an individual whose mark we can recognise by some indefinable nuance. Even children can feel the difference between a well- written book and that of an author who uses language unimaginatively.
>
> (Colwell 2000, 107)

This is not to suggest that picture books cannot also be educational. One interviewee who was also an early literacy educator talked about the difficulty in finding texts that contained elements that could be used in teaching:

> We wanted to find a certain picture book that had words that allowed us to model that with the kids, about how you would stop and look at the word and then use certain clues to then predict what the word might mean, and things like that. So I was really interested in picture books for that reason and I sort of saw where there were gaps as well with certain strategies that we found are quite tricky to find the right kind of book. . . . You might have a reading lesson where you really just want to look at specific digraphs like 'th' or 'sh' and you want a book that's got good examples of that, you know, and often it's not in books that you'd find at the bookstore; it's in books that are produced by educational companies. [Participant 10]

This respondent also considered how each book is distinct and enjoyed for very different reasons:

> If you can combine a good narrative with those other literacy things too that we're looking for, of course that's fantastic. But you know sometimes you do just want a great story with a good problem and, you know, a nice resolution. And you can use those in other classes too. Especially in writing we use them as mentor texts and . . . it shows kids how a story develops. [Participant 10]

When considering Colwell's quote above, there could be a degree of flexibility in how texts are presented to readers of trade picture books compared with educational picture books, with the educational picture book consciously embedding early literacy examples and the trade picture books not. The production values of the trade picture book also set it apart from the educational via its physical paratextual features. These physical features are often developed for their gift element, hence the additional cost:

> It works to either entertain or enable a conversation about a particular topic. And then at another level picture books function as gifts: the picture book market relies heavily on a kind of gift exchange because they are often more expensive than other children's books. [Participant 11]

Clearly, then, the educational children's book, with its focus on learning more than linear narratives, and with reference-like features, can in fact enhance the reading experience for children if delivered in digital format. This has been observed in the research noted in Chapter 2 where the enhancements can improve comprehension in cases where the AR does not disrupt the storyline (Delneshin et al. 2020). The only exception to this would be the emerging popularity of the audiobook, which, for children's picture books, is not only an aural experience but one that can be delivered online via a real reader. Essentially, this mimics the act of an adult-mediated text, which raises questions about whether it is, in fact, considered digital, as one of the interviewees explained about Story Box:

> We do have deals with Story Box Library and the ABC so that they can, and those are not exclusive deals, so that they can create kind of digital versions that blend the ebook and audio track to make . . . that book accessible. [Participant 11]
>
> If we're talking about the digital picture book, watching a video of someone reading the book, that's an interesting kind of in between. Like I don't know . . . if you have an author reading through their own book, so a child's watching that, is that better than flicking through a digital book with buttons? [Participant 1]

This last statement is an interesting one to consider since the pandemic lockdowns, which saw libraries mostly closed and borrowing for picture books impacted. The success of subscription-based platforms such as Story Box indicated that read-aloud storybooks were in demand still, and that in the event of parents not being able to read stories to their children on a regular basis, and with homeschooling perhaps preventing these kinds of interactions, video-delivered audiobooks became a format of preference. The other interesting thing to note about this last comment is that it emphasises the importance of the adult as a mediator for a children's picture-book text, whether that be via a static pre-recording or in person. However, the research would suggest opportunities for exploring paratextual elements of a book, and the architecture of a book, are greatly reduced in any digital format. Because these features are what is so cherished about picture books, including the ways in which they facilitate parent/child interaction, children's picture-book creators will continue to resist digital productions.

While it is commendable that publishers support continuation of the physical picture book, it is with the intention of it being delivered by a literate and at least somewhat entertaining adult reader. Additionally, it is with the intention that all children have access to physical picture books and that those children navigate the picture book as an abled child.

References

Bai, Jie, Hui Zhang, Qian Chen, Xiulan Cheng, and Yun Zhou. 2022. "Technical Supports and Emotional Design in Digital Picture Books for Children: A Review." *Procedia Computer Science* 201: 174–80. https://doi.org/10.1016/j.procs.2022.03.025.

Books+Publishing. 2023. "Nielson: Australia Book Sales Up 7.2% in 2022." www.booksandpublishing.com.au/articles/2023/01/17/225222/nielsen-australian-book-sales-up-7-2-in-2022/.

Braun, Virginia, and Victoria Clarke. 2006. "Using Thematic Analysis in Psychology." *Qualitative Research in Psychology* 3 (2): 77–101. https://doi.org/10.1191/1478088706qp063oa.

Colwell, Eileen. 2000. *Once Upon a Time*. Hebden Bridge: Pennine Pens.

Delneshin, Danaei, Hamid R. Jamali, Yazdan Mansourian, and Hassan Rastegarpour. 2020. "Comparing Reading Comprehension Between Children Reading Augmented Reality and Print Storybooks." *Computers & Education* 153 (August): 1–10. https://doi.org/10.1016/j.compedu.2020.103900.

DePaolo, Concetta A., and Kelly Wilkinson. 2014. "Get Your Head into the Clouds: Using Word Clouds for Analyzing Qualitative Assessment Data." *TechTrends* 58 (April): 38–44. https://doi.org/10.1007/s11528-014-0750-9.

Driscoll, Beth, and Susannah Bowen. 2022. "White, Female, and High Rates of Mental Illness: New Diversity Research Offers a Snapshot of the Publishing Industry." *The Conversation*, August 31. https://theconversation.com/white-female-and-high-rates-of-mental-illness-new-diversity-research-offers-a-snapshot-of-the-publishing-industry-189679.

Ellis, Carolyn S., and Arthur P. Bochner. 2006. "Analyzing Analytic Autoethnography: An Autopsy." *Journal of Contemporary Ethnography* 35 (4): 429–49. https://doi.org/10.1177/0891241606286979.

Furenes, May Irene, Natalia Kucirkova, and Adriana G. Bus. 2021. "A Comparison of Children's Reading on Paper Versus Screen: A Meta-Analysis." *Review of Educational Research* 91 (4): 483–517. https://doi.org/10.3102/003465432199807.

Growing Up in Australia. 2014. "Growing Up in Australia: The Longitudinal Study of Australian Children (LSAC)." Accessed July 20, 2023. https://growingupinaustralia.gov.au/.

IBIS World. 2023. "Book Publishing in Australia: Market Size, Industry Analysis, Trends and Forecasts (2023–2028)." Accessed December 10, 2023. www.ibisworld.com/au/industry/book-publishing/171/#IndustryStatisticsAndTrends.

Kirkus Reviews. 2011. "The Heart and the Bottle: An Interactive Book." *Kirkus Reviews*. Accessed September 10, 2023. www.kirkusreviews.com/book-reviews/oliver-jeffers/heart-and-bottle-app/.

Lyon Clark, Beverly. 2003. *Kiddie Lit: The Cultural Construction of Children's Literature in America*. Baltimore: Johns Hopkins University Press.

McNair, Jonda C. 2021. "Surprise, Surprise! Exploring Dust Jackets, Case Covers, and Endpapers in Picture Books to Support Comprehension." *The Reading Teacher* 74 (4): 363–73. https://doi.org/10.1002/trtr.1985.

Mol, Suzanne E., and Adriana G. Bus. 2011. "To Read or Not to Read: A Meta-Analysis of Print Exposure from Infancy to Early Adulthood." *Psychological Bulletin* 137 (2): 267–96.

Nolan, Sybil, Katherine Day, Wonsun Shin, and Wilfred Wang. 2022. "Books Versus Screens: A Study of Australian Children's Media Use During the COVID Pandemic." *Publishing Research Quarterly* 38, no. 4 (December): 749–59. https://doi.org/10.1007/s12109-022-09899-w.

Pace, Steven. 2012. "Writing the Self into Research: Using Grounded Theory Analytic Strategies in Autoethnography." *TEXT Special Issue: Creativity:*

Cognitive, Social and Cultural Perspectives, edited by Nigel McLoughlin and Donna Lee Brien 16 (13). https://doi.org/10.52086/001c.31147.

Pantaleo, Sylvia 2003. "Godzilla lives in New York: Grade 1 students and the peritextual features of picture books." *Journal of Children's Literature* 29(2): 66–76.

Sipe, Lawrence R., and Anne E. Brightman. 2009. "Young Children's Interpretations of Page Breaks in Contemporary Picture Storybooks." *Journal of Literacy Research* 41 (1): 68–103. https://doi.org/10.1080/10862960802695214.

Strouse, Gabrielle A., and Patricia A. Ganea. 2017. "A Print Book Preference: Caregivers Report Higher Child Enjoyment and More Adult – Child Interactions When Reading Print Than Electronic Books." *International Journal of Child-Computer Interaction* 12 (April): 8–15. https://doi.org/10.1016/j.ijcci.2017.02.001.

Wei, Chun-Chun, and Min-Yuan Ma. 2020. "Designing Attractive Children's Picture Books: Evaluating the Attractiveness Factors of Various Picture Book Formats." *Design Journal* 23 (2): 287–308. https://doi.org/10.1080/14606925.2020.1718277.

West, Elizabeth. 2022. *The Women Who Invented Twentieth-Century Children's Literature: Only the Best*. New York: Routledge. https://doi.org/10.4324/9781003306870.

4 Conclusion

Often when we think of picture books, we tend to have memories of being read to by an adult, and that the format for the picture book is often a hardback with an enticing image on the front cover, maybe a jacket and luxurious stock from which the internal illustrations spring from the pages. Perhaps those memories are of the bedtime story, which is an entrenched and much-loved practice in many families, or maybe it was that a schoolteacher would often read a text aloud in class while everyone sat cross-legged on the mat. Given the prominence of texts as part of many children's upbringings (at home, at school or elsewhere), and the importance of early literacy to a child's learning and ability to thrive (Growing Up in Australia 2014), it's likely that the scenarios described here would apply for most readers.

The tactility of the picture book reminds us that, historically, it has made a significant journey to a genre quite separate to adult literature and special in its own right. This Brass Age of children's literature, between the 1930s and the 1960s, heralded the beginning of the picture book as art form (West 2023), spurred on by women in the publishing industry who wanted to elevate the quality of children's reading material in line with a new interest in child psychology (West 2023, 98). The popularity of children's books also impacted the present features and qualities that we associate with these childhood memories and experiences: the large, full-page illustrations, their artistic attributes, paratextual elements such as endpapers and jackets. As noted by McNair (2021), Sipe and Brightman (2009) and Pantaleo (2016), the paratextual features of picture books have offered a variety of ways to experience the picture book separate to the text, mostly guided by the adult reader. Certainly, the research suggests when adults mediate the reading experience, children absorb and comprehend the texts more successfully. Often this is because they enjoy the reading experience more when it is delivered by an adult. However, as was found in the research conducted for this book, not all children are read to by an adult. What about children for whom access to books is not easy, or too expensive? The COVID-19 lockdowns exposed the disparity

Conclusion   45

between shared reading time in families that read together and, in some cases, increased reading to their children and those families that reduced shared reading time in favour of other activities. Or families that perhaps utilised more predominantly educational digital texts. The sense of nostalgia for picture books, therefore, might need to be challenged.

The study presented in this book sought to assess publishers' perceptions of picture books in the contemporary landscape, and to explore a gap in our knowledge of how picture-book publishers cater to diverse readerships and new reading platforms in the digital age. In answering the questions in the first chapter of this book, the greater proportion of the Australian children's picture-book market is still physical, and this was rigorously supported and defended by most of the picture-book producers and users interviewed. While there has been some experimentation with digital features and design, the impact of these digital augmentations on narrative is considered disruptive on many levels: to the format as a physical object to be coveted; as an impingement on the shared reading experience because the child can be guided by the device; and as a distraction from a narrative that has to be read in a certain way and is designed to be read from front cover to back cover, page by page. Many of the respondents mentioned how the limitations of the digital format also impacted on the artistic features of the storybook quite simply via the size of the device – the artistry of the illustrations couldn't be appreciated on an iPad, for example. But it is also the prohibitive cost of a digital design that could go above and beyond a simple PDF that prevents publishers from exploring this space. Therefore, when it comes to engaging with digital texts, children have simply not been given enough good examples to do so. While they can access PDF versions of picture-book texts, usually from their local libraries, they can also borrow physical formats, and parents encourage borrowing physical texts over digital.

While it is ideal that children are read to from an early age, and that children who observe their parents enjoying reading as a pastime tend to also become readers (Smith 2021), not all parents have an appreciation for literature, for themselves or their children; in some cases parents might have low literacy levels, or might not understand the architecture of a good picture book enough to help the child navigate it. Much of the research around paratextual features, for example, is presented on the assumption that parents will also explore endpapers and page turns, and that they will discuss these features with children. As one respondent in this study observed, it is essential that children be taught how to navigate a physical book – it isn't necessarily intrinsically understood. What if nobody shows them? Additionally, how does a physical picture book help a child who might read differently, such as a child who requires specific assistance, if they don't have a parent to guide them?

The emergence of platforms such as Story Box have seemingly brought the digital together with the physical. Albeit a static delivery, the reader can still engage with the picture book as if in real time while the child listens to the reading and watches the reader point out the various features of the picture-book text without disrupting the narrative flow. Also, the readings can be delivered by a celebrity or someone who has skill in delivering the text in an entertaining way. While it is not clear whether Story Box or platforms like it were considered a digital format, the reception of audio for children's picture books is an interesting area ripe for further investigation. Publishers do not offer audiobook versions for single publications for an obvious reason: the expense is disproportionate to the reading time. However, as a collection, these platforms offer a suite of readings, and another income stream for authors and illustrators. While most publishers allowed authors to read their texts on YouTube during the pandemic lockdowns, this practice has been rejected since and transformed to more profitable agreements between publishers and third parties.

Educational texts, however, are perceived quite differently and many readers are responsive to digital educational texts. This is because an educational text is not seen as an art form; rather, its qualities are steeped in learning activities like listening, referencing, repeating and responding to prompts. Many educational texts are also explicitly embedded with early learning literary structures and tools, which are mostly implicit in trade picture books. Also, while trade books are often seen as 'gift-like', educational texts do not garner the same appreciation for production qualities. It is their engagement level that is seen as advantageous. In this way, they can be read independently, but also parents and caregivers prefer them to be read independently because they are designed to be both entertaining and utilitarian. It is likely, therefore, that engagement with educational texts will not be a shared reading experience between parent and child. The physical picture-book experience, then, becomes even more pronounced for its shared practice.

Although some countries are changing their laws to align national legislation with the European Accessibility Act – a requirement that was passed in 2022 and will come into full effect by 2025 (such as in Italy) – these laws have not been mandated for trade picture-book texts. Because picture books are considered an antidote to screentime, they are, as one respondent pointed out, 'sacrosanct' and works of art. Illustrations should be given their due for the specific skill that book illustration demands of the artist. Some of the most loved and well-known texts are examples of artistic flair, but with an impressive measure of consistency and proportion as well as the artist's ability to capture movement through line and colour, and the picture books' necessary emotional expression in each character. As Anthony Browne states: 'The illustration in children's books are the first paintings most children see, and because of that they are incredibly important. What we see and share at that age stays with us for life' (Browne in Hunt 2009, Foreword).

But this aching sense of nostalgia that binds us to the children's book genre must continue to be challenged, perhaps. It may forestall the inevitable, and what might be a positive enhancement in the picture-book sector, if we continue to frame the picture book as an 'art form', as more tactile, and always showcased in a different way from how a book chapter might be experienced – face out, the cover admired. Consider the delight of features that would have once been the 'gimmick': flaps, die-cuts and other paper features embedded in the text. How do these compare with the AI embedded in a picture-book app that might allow you to open the cupboards in a child's room, make snow fall or lions roar? How can we enable publishers to explore how augmented digital texts can complement narratives and elevate artists' work? To covet a book is a powerful nod to the emotional connection we have with picture-book texts, and why we perhaps appear reluctant to abandon its magnetic appeal. But this connection is reserved for those who have the means to purchase them, too; it also favours the privilege of access and engagement. It is therefore imperative that we find avenues to financially support authors, publishers and illustrators to explore ways that the traditional and the digital can complement each other.

References

Growing Up in Australia. 2014. "Growing Up in Australia: The Longitudinal Study of Australian Children (LSAC)." Accessed July 20, 2023. https://growingupinaustralia.gov.au/.

Hunt, Peter. 2009. *Illustrated Children's Books*. London: Black Dog Press.

McNair, Jonda C. 2021. "Surprise, Surprise! Exploring Dust Jackets, Case Covers, and Endpapers in Picture Books to Support Comprehension." *The Reading Teacher* 74 (4): 363–73. https://doi.org/10.1002/trtr.1985.

Nolan, Sybil, Katherine Day, Wonsun Shin, and Wilfred Wang. 2022. "Books Versus Screens: A Study of Australian Children's Media Use During the COVID Pandemic." *Publishing Research Quarterly* 38, no. 4 (December): 749–59. https://doi.org/10.1007/s12109-022-09899-w.

Pantaleo, Sylvia. 2016. "Primary Students' Understanding and Appreciation of the Artwork in Picturebooks." *Journal of Early Childhood Literacy* 16 (2): 228–55. https://doi.org/10.1177/1468798415569816.

Sipe, Lawrence R., and Anne E. Brightman. 2009. "Young Children's Interpretations of Page Breaks in Contemporary Picture Storybooks." *Journal of Literacy Research* 41 (1): 68–103. https://doi.org/10.1080/10862960802695214.

Smith, Claire. 2021. "Reading in the Time of the Pandemic." *DKG Bulletin: Collegial Exchange* 88 (2): 35–37. https://research.ebsco.com/c/xppotz/viewer/pdf/w42asonunn.

West, Elizabeth. 2023. *The Women Who Invented Twentieth-Century Children's Literature: Only the Best*. New York: Routledge. https://doi.org/10.4324/9781003306870.

Index

accessibility and inclusion 13–15, 25, 30–1, 44; access to digital books 6, 14–15, 25, 29–32, 44–5; book prices and 30–2, 44; children in remote areas 14, 29, 31; children with disability 14, 29, 31; diverse readerships 29, 45; *see also* audiobook editions of picture books; European Accessibility Act 2019; Story Box Library

adult mediation of picture books *see* parent/carer mediation of digital picture books; parent/carer mediation of physical picture books

Allen & Unwin, children's list 4; Dromkeen Medal 4

Allen, Pamela, author/illustrator 4

art form of physical children's books 4–5, 21–2, 27, 34–5, 44–6; artistic and production values 5, 22–3, 25, 29, 33, 44, 46; best read aloud 12, 21–7; creative vision and commercial pressures 27–9; design for adults as buyers 24, 28; design privileged by publishers 5, 12, 28; digitalisation influence on 29, 45, 46; esteemed less in some literary circles 4–5; historical influence on 5, 27; tactile, tangible art form 2, 6, 21–2, 35, 44–5; *see also* page breaks in physical books; peritext and paratext

artificial intelligence (AI) and books *see* augmented reality (AR) in digital picture books

audiobook editions of picture books 13, 30, 32, 41, 46; substitute for parent/carer mediation 13, 30, 41, 46; video-delivery preferred 41; *see also* accessibility and inclusion; Story Box Library

augmented reality (AR) in digital picture books 6, 9–10, 40; *see also* digital picture book interactive features

Australian picture book publishing, history 3–4

authors 28, 47; and audiobooks 41, 46; and Children's Book Council of Australia 5; publishers' children's lists 4; and understanding of children's expectations 27; writing style 39–40; *see also* collaboration in picture book publishing; Story Box Library; writing for physical books

Barnard, Peggy, author 3
Base, Graeme, author/illustrator 4
Blinky Bill series, by Dorothy Wall 3
Bluey series 28
Blyton, Enid, author 27
book borrowing *see* libraries
book sales, Australia, children's titles 5, 34

bookstores 23, 34, 40; bricks-and-mortar 28, 31, 34–5, 38; discount department stores (DDS) 25, 28–9, 31; online 28
Brass Age (1930 to 1960), UK 5, 44
Brooks, Ron, author 4
buying children's picture books *see* market and market trends for picture books

Children's Book Council of Australia (CBCA) Awards 3–4; criticism of judgement capabilities 4; history 3; positive influence of 4–5
children's preferences for picture book formats 6, 8, 12
collaboration in picture book publishing 20, 47; creator-publisher relationship 4, 21; and specialist editorial skills 4, 5, 20–1
COVID-19 lockdowns and: access to digital books 30–1, 41; audiobook use 14, 41; book buying and sales 1, 5, 31, 34–5; children's digital device use 1, 13, 37; compulsory homeschooling 1, 3, 13, 41; *see also* audiobook editions of picture books; libraries; Story Box Library
creative vision and commercial pressures 27–9

Denton, Terry, illustrator 4
digital device use and children: apps, games, videos predominant 12, 36–7, 39; increased use during and since lockdowns 1, 13, 37; *see also* reading and gaming as distinctive digital device uses
digital picture book interactive features 10, 12, 36, 38–9, 41, 45; cost and technical limitations on use of 10, 45; as distractions 9, 10, 33, 38–9; *see also* narrative
digital picture books: digital technology levels differ in 10;

European Accessibility Act 2019 and quality of 14–15, 46; impact on learning questioned 32; publishers do not prioritise 2, 36; publishers' limited expertise in 34, 35–6; publishers' low investment in resources for 10, 36; publishers' resistance to 36, 39, 41; and quality of standalone editions 12, 15, 29; *see also* augmented reality (AR) in digital picture books; educational books; market and market trends for picture books; physical picture books reproduced as PDFs
discount department stores (DDS) *see* bookstores
Dromkeen Estate 3; collection at State Library of Victoria 3–4; Dromkeen Medal 3

educational books 38–41, 46; digital formats 2, 5, 29, 39, 40–1; educational and picture book publishing differ 38–41; narratives with educational value 5, 13, 27, 38–41, 45–6
engagement, enjoyment, or entertainment and: audiobooks 14, 46; digital picture books 2, 9–10, 12, 45; digital versus physical books 20, 36; *see also* parent/carer mediation of digital picture books; parent/carer mediation of physical picture books; physical picture books (traditional format)
e-readers: launched 8; and predicted demise of physical book 8
European Accessibility Act 2019 14–15, 46

Fox, Mem, author 4

gaming and reading *see* reading and gaming as distinctive digital device uses

Gibbs, May, author/illustrator 3
Gumnut Baby series, by May Gibbs 3

Hawkins, Sheila, illustrator 3
The Heart and the Bottle, by Oliver Jeffers 39
Hobbs, Leigh, author 4

illustration: in digital picture books 34, 45; in physical picture books 3–5, 20–1, 34–5, 44, 46–7; and text skilfully combined 4, 5, 21, 33; visual appeal of physical picture books 5, 20–1, 33
inclusion and accessibility *see* accessibility and inclusion
independent bookstores *see* bookstores
independent reading 25–6, 39, 46
Ingpen, Robert, illustrator 4; Hans Christian Anderson Medal recipient 4

Jeffers, Oliver, author 39

learning and: audiobooks 13; digital books 9, 10, 36, 38; physical books 10, 30, 44; *see also* educational books; peritext; paratext
Lester, Alison, author/illustrator 4
librarians 4, 27, 38
libraries: book borrowing 1, 14, 19, 31, 41, 45; creative programs during pandemic 13; *see also* COVID-19 lockdowns; school libraries; Story Box Library
Lindsay, Norman, author/illustrator 3
listening and being read to: children and picture books 10, 23, 25
literacy and picture books 2, 10–12, 40, 44–5; audiobooks and 13; *see also* learning
Lu Reeves Archives 3

The Magic Pudding, by Norman Lindsay 3
market and market trends for picture books: adults as buyers 22, 24–36, 40, 47; affordability of picture books 24–5; commercial, cost, and price pressures on publishers 27–9; as gifts 25, 40, 46; impact of low sales for digital books 34–6; market preference for physical books 34–5; small market and publisher decisions 10, 27; *see also* bookstores
meta narrative of picture books 22, 26

narrative 2, 10, 20, 39, 40; digital books and 6, 32, 38; narrative thread lost in digital books 9, 33, 38–9, 45; physical books and 2, 21, 31–3, 40; *see also* educational books
National Centre for Australian Children's Literature (NCACL) 3; and Lu Reeves Archives 3

Oldmeadow, Court and Joyce 3; *see also* Dromkeen Estate

page breaks in physical books 11, 12, 22–3, 45
page turns *see* page breaks in physical books
paratext *see* peritext and paratext
parent/carer mediation of digital picture books 10, 29, 32–3, 41; and book buying 10, 31
parent/carer mediation of physical picture books 2, 27, 32, 36–7, 41, 44; bonding, shared parent-child experience 8, 13, 20–4, 27, 35, 37–9, 45–6; and book buying 24, 27; reading as performance 12, 22, 26, 40–1, 46; *see also* learning; parents as unavailable or reluctant readers; parents' reading and effect on children's learning

Index

parents as unavailable or reluctant readers 23, 26, 36–7, 45
parents prefer physical books 12–13, 32, 37–9, 45; memories influence preference 44; preference challenged 45
parents' reading and effect on children's learning 13, 26, 30, 32, 44; cognitive development 8; literary skills 8, 40; reception of texts 10; text comprehension 8–10, 30, 40, 44; text processing 8, 40; *see also* learning
PDF editions *see* physical picture books reproduced as PDFs
Penguin Books, Puffin Australia imprint 4
peritext and paratext: paratext in picture books 10–12, 20–4, 33, 38, 40–1, 44; parent/carer awareness of paratext 9–10, 21–3, 26; parent/carer awareness of peritext 10–11; peritext of physical books 24
physical picture books (traditional format): as antidote to screen time 2, 12–13, 36–9; best read aloud 12, 21–7; disadvantage and access to 25–6, 30; esteemed less in some literary circles 4; history, Australia 3–5; and increased children's engagement 2, 11; positive impact on learning 8, 10, 32; *see also* art form of physical children's books; educational books; illustration; narrative; parent/carer mediation of physical picture books
physical picture books reproduced as PDFs 2, 5, 10, 15, 27, 33–5, 45
picture book and educational publishing differ 5, 38–41
Pilsener, Dave, author 28
publishers of children's picture books: creator-publisher relationship 4; digital expertise limited 34–6; and digitally engaged children 2; disregard for digitality-story relationship 6; physical book expertise of 2, 34, 37–8; publishing digital books 2, 5, 8, 15, 39; small, overworked publishing teams 34–5; and specialist editorial skills 4, 5, 21; *see also* picture book and educational publishing differ; women in Australian children's book publishing
publishers prefer physical picture books 1, 5, 29–30, 34–5, 45; preference challenged 31–2, 45
Puffin Australia: children's list initiated by Julie Watts, OAM 4; Dromkeen Medal recipient 4

quality and children's literature 3–4, 11–12, 19, 27–9, 35, 45

reading and gaming as distinctive digital device uses 2, 6, 10, 12, 20, 33, 36–9
Reeves, Lu, collector of children's books 3
research methodology for this book 19–20

school libraries 4, 14; *see also* Story Box Library
schools 4; and creative programming during pandemic 13
Smith, Craig, illustrator 4
State Library of Victoria and Dromkeen collection 3
Story Box Library 29–30, 41, 46; and COVID lockdowns 14; and limited library access 14; similar to parental/carer mediation 30, 46
story *see* narrative

text *see* writing for physical books
text and illustration *see* illustration
trade publishing *see* publishers of children's picture books

Wall, Dorothy 3
Wang, Gabrielle, author/illustrator 4
Watts, Julie, OAM, author and publisher 3
Wild, Margaret, author 4
Wish and the Magic Nut, by Peggy Barnard, illus. Sheila Hawkins 3
women in Australian children's book publishing 4–5; continuing predominance of 4–5, 20, 27; historical influence of 5, 27, 44; pejorative perceptions of 4–5; specialist editorial skills of 5, 20–1
writing for physical books 29, 40; adult engagement with 25, 27, 30; and children's engagement with literary texts 2, 8; quality of 39–40, 46; *see also* illustration; narrative
writing style *see* writing for physical books

For Product Safety Concerns and Information please contact our EU representative GPSR@taylorandfrancis.com
Taylor & Francis Verlag GmbH, Kaufingerstraße 24, 80331 München, Germany

www.ingramcontent.com/pod-product-compliance
Lightning Source LLC
Chambersburg PA
CBHW071823230426
43670CB00013B/2555